ILLUSION DWELLER

ILLUSION
DWELLER

· · · · · ·

THE CLIMBING LIFE OF
STIMSON BULLITT

STIMSON BULLITT

Foreword by TOM HORNBEIN

Introduction by JOEL CONNELLY

**MOUNTAINEERS
BOOKS**

Mountaineers Books is the nonprofit publishing division of The Mountaineers, an organization founded in 1906 and dedicated to the exploration, preservation, and enjoyment of outdoor and wilderness areas.

MOUNTAINEERS BOOKS

1001 SW Klickitat Way, Suite 201 • Seattle, WA 98134
800.553.4453 • www.mountaineersbooks.org

Printed in the United States of America
Distributed in the United Kingdom by Cordee, www.cordee.co.uk

16 15 14 13   1 2 3 4 5

Copy Editor: Sherri Shultz
Developmental Editors: Jenna Free and Phyllis Hatfield
Book Design: Mountaineers Books
Cover and Layout: John Barnett / 4 Eyes Design
Cover Photo: *Stimson Bullitt, an octogenarian rock climber, scales a difficult 5.10 crack.*
        © Cliff Leight / Aurora Photos

Library of Congress Cataloging-in-Publication Data

Bullitt, Stimson.
  Illusion dweller : the climbing life of Stimson Bullitt / by Stimson Bullitt.
    pages cm
  Includes index.
  ISBN 978-1-59485-860-4 (hc) -- ISBN 978-1-59485-774-4 (pbk) -- ISBN 978-1-59485-824-6 (ebook) 1. Bullitt, Stimson. 2. Mountaineers--United States--Biography. I. Title.
  GV199.92.B85A3 2013
  796.522092--dc23
  [B]

                    2013020311

♻ Printed on 30% post-consumer waste recycled paper

ISBN (hardcover): 978-1-59485-860-4
ISBN (paperback): 978-1-59485-774-4
ISBN (ebook): 978-1-59485-824-6

Dedicated to Tina Bullitt

CONTENTS

PUBLISHER'S NOTE

· · · · ·

THE STRUCTURE OF THIS MOUNTAINEERING memoir follows to a large degree Stimson Bullitt's own outline, which reflected his wide-ranging knowledge, interests, and experiences. An exceptionally active outdoorsman, he was also exceptionally learned—once called by an admirer "the Monsieur Montaigne of Seattle." He studded his prose with quotations from the ancient Greek and Roman philosophers all the way through to contemporary writers of fiction such as Alice Munro. A lawyer and community activist, he thought deeply about public policy. The introduction to this book by Joel Connelly provides a fuller picture of Stimson's life and all that he contributed to his larger community.

This volume, based on extensive manuscript pages left behind at Stimson's death in 2009 at age eighty-nine, focuses on his remarkable climbing endeavors. Stimson always was drawn to the mountains of his native western Washington. But it was not until he reached his fifties and sixties that he sought challenges on summits of numerous formidable peaks, including Denali and Mount Rainier. And then, at age seventy, he took up rock climbing—a pure and painful obsession that became a match and foil for his inner demons. This book's title, *Illusion Dweller*, refers to a particularly hardearned and difficult climb at Joshua Tree when Stimson was eighty-three.

The Mountaineers Books is grateful to Tina Bullitt and Stimson's literary executor, David Brewster, for bringing the manuscript to our attention and offering their support and insight. Tom Hornbein, a devoted friend and climbing partner, also offered advice and encouragement throughout our editing process, and provides further context for Stimson's climbing life in his foreword.

Stimson Bullitt rock-climbed until just short of his death, and his achievements serve as inspiration to climbers of any age—and to anyone striving to kindle a spirit of adventure as they grow older. Through his investigations of climbing, risk, and challenge, these writings illuminate still more of the rich life of the body and mind that Stimson pursued.

FOREWORD

· · · · ·

I CAN IMAGINE THAT SPECIAL twinkle in Stimson Bullitt's eyes as he muses that his words continue to touch our lives nearly half a decade after the final beat of his heart. *Illusion Dweller*, a labor of love of his later years, was created to share with us not only his affair with mountains but also his reflections on what it all meant—the challenge, the risk, the trade-offs, the companionship, the pleasure of suffering, the heroes. This book is a precious part of Stim's immortality.

Mountains in their varied garbs and seductions were a foundation for much else in Stim's other lives as lawyer, civic leader, caretaker of wilderness. They were a constant that stirred his passions and fueled his dreams. *Illusion Dweller* captures a good bit of that relationship as he recounts his adventures wandering high hills with his children, with his climbing companions, and often with just himself.

I see two stages in Stim's exploration of high places (and himself). In the first he wandered as a free and somewhat naïve spirit, uninformed and too little troubled by the darker moods and hidden hazards of his playground. He was blissfully unaware of or unconcerned with the techniques and attendant paraphernalia that come with the mountaineering game. His accounts of some of these solo moments make one's palms sweat. Blessed with guts and not a little luck to offset his lack of experience-based judgment, he survived these introductory years reasonably intact, entering stage two at an age when many are hanging it up and moving their aging bodies into more comfortable, risk-averse lifestyles.

Stim approached climbing with total, damn-the-torpedoes commitment. On his first attempt (of three) to climb Mount McKinley in 1978, it took the determined action of his two companions, Bill Sumner and Jim Wickwire, to turn his exhausted but summit-bound body around. This intensity of commitment once the battle was joined would continue throughout his climbing life, crowned in a sense by the climb from which this book derives its title. He made a number of trips from Seattle to Joshua Tree National Park before he finally succeeded in leading this strenuous pitch. Even at eighty-three, it was a challenge he could not otherwise put to rest.

Like most of us who climb, Stim pursued this mostly healthful addiction for a mixture of reasons, including the beauty and solitude of wild places, companionship, and exploring the unknown (including that within himself). More than most, though, Stim candidly singles out the need to prove himself: "The motive for continuing to climb to the limit of my capacity seems to dwell in a never-ending urge to compensate for prior failure to sufficiently excel at demanding athletics . . . an excessive concern with proving my manhood to myself."

Stim pushed right to the edge, sometimes a tad beyond. A climb of a route called Outer Space on Snow Creek Wall left him, having missed on a desperate lunge move on the crux, with a broken ankle and a challenging, painful descent back to the car. This sort of outcome was not a rare occurrence: "Except for the punctured lung, ligaments and frost bite, all my mountaineering injuries were broken bones. . . ."

The latter chapters of this book (chapters 5, 6, and 7) are for me the lode where Stim has mined golden lessons from a life of mountain adventure. He reflects on lessons learned from observation, not least of his own behaviors, touching on many elements of the mountain experience including seductions and hazards, companionship and solo wandering, and heroes, but coming back again and again to risk in its various flavors—a topic on which he is more qualified than most to opine. With an ingenuous integrity, he often cites his own near misses (and a few hits) as examples of what not to do. The reflective Stim is his own harshest critic.

Some of his friends were convinced Stim Bullitt might gain *Guinness Book of Records* fame by being the oldest person to end his life falling off a mountain. We were wrong. As Stim's body grew old and his stamina waned, he moved from endurance mountaineering to the sprint of sport climbing. He climbed on the walls at the Vertical World, a local rock-climbing gym where he, Bill Sumner, Brownie Schoene, and I gathered regularly to chat and climb. By virtue of intense, focused commitment, he willed his body to accomplish impressive physical feats. Competition in that setting, as in his early boxing years, was an attraction. He enjoyed the periodic contests at the climbing gym, where he always came in first in his age group, and I second (at the time there were only two of us in the old guys' class).

I will now leave Stim's world of high adventure and risk, as did Stim not so long ago as both diminishing memory and physical capacity compelled. You can imagine the crater that opened when climbing became reminiscences. Each time we were together, he would briefly, with a sad smile, reflect upon the loss. Then we would move on to other topics. Our times of climbing together served as a foundation on which was built a whole world of insatiable exploration of topics—why one climbs, risk as an essential dietary constituent, whether heroes still matter as we grow older, contemplation of life's final chapters and how to make them a worthy adventure. Precious were gatherings around the Bullitt table by candlelight, especially on New Year's Eve, with the richness of gently lubricated conversation and a unique table, followed by adjourning to seats around the fire to explore literature, poetry, or unknown mountains hiding in our minds.

In those final months before Stim died, when his short-term memory no longer provided an effective belay, an ineffable peace and simple joy in being with friends seemed to take over. I wondered whether the inability to climb might also have helped free him from that unrelenting pressure to prove himself; his illness simply flipped the switch and turned off the quest that had driven him for so long.

At the closing moment of this memoir, two illusion dwellers—a bit of seductive rock and its human protagonist—fuse into one last ultimate declaration of the value of illusion in fulfilling dreams, and the magic wrought when dreams and determination meet.

Tom Hornbein
August 2013

INTRODUCTION

• • • • •

The Achieving Life of Stimson Bullitt

THE AGED BLUE WEBSTER'S DICTIONARY on my desk carries a simple inscription: "Stimson Bullitt, April 1943."

The dictionary was one of fifty books its owner took to the War of the Pacific. He went to fight the Japanese after defending the Nisei at home. Before shipping out, he wrote Washington State's congressional delegation to urge that Japanese American soldiers in the US Army be "sent to whatever fighting fronts there are or may be to the east of us."

The dictionary went ashore with Stim Bullitt in the invasion of the Philippines at Leyte, where in a shorebound landing craft he was struck by a piece of shrapnel. It remained in his right shoulder until his death. Typically, Stim told daughter Dorothy that shrapnel was "an easy way to get a Purple Heart." He underplayed the kamikaze attacks offshore, and the sight of distant flashes from the eighteen-inch guns of Japan's mighty battleship *Yamato* in the battle of Leyte Gulf.

Stim Bullitt was Seattle's most self-deprecatory achiever.

He headed a Northwest broadcast empire. He successfully practiced appellate law. He ran twice for Congress in the 1950s and wrote an acclaimed book *(To Be a Politician)* inspired by the experience. He gave land that became a splendid state park in the Issaquah Alps, and turned dilapidated buildings into residential towers and Harbor Steps Park on Seattle's First Avenue.

He climbed 20,320-foot Mount McKinley at sixty-two as well as scaled 18,490-foot Pico de Orizaba in Mexico, the continent's third-highest peak. He did the north side of 9,415-foot Mount Stuart—"a big deal," in Seattle climber Jim Wickwire's words—at age seventy-nine, and stopped climbing only at age eighty-seven.

The achieving life almost ended years earlier. In his memoir *River Dark and Bright,* Stim Bullitt owned up to "black despair" that had him "brooding over suicide" for seven years during his forties. He cursed the "sense of duty" that kept him from ending his life, but gradually the inner debate over "to go on living or not" dwindled.

The experience of being trapped at 12,900 feet on Mount Rainier's Liberty Ridge, convinced he was going to die—he wrote out a note giving instructions to one of his sisters—awakened Stim to the value of life. "The Liberty Ridge episode and its aftermath taught me two lessons," he later wrote, "notable because they endured. First, I was touched by expressions of concern and relief by relatives, friends, and acquaintances in letters, phone calls, and stops on the street. Discovering their affection was gratifying because I had thought myself unseen . . . The other lesson was to relish the pleasures of each day, delighting in this process that had come to seem so precious. It made me [so] savor life that not even turning sixty a month later could sink me into deep gloom."

He had a steel core beneath his genteel reserve and civility. The manners came from his mother, King Broadcasting founder Dorothy Bullitt. He followed her as president of a broadcast empire that believed in public service. But whether it was boxing when he was young, or doing moves on the climbing wall at REI in his eighties, Stim Bullitt engaged in a lifelong effort to prove himself to himself. His greatest demonstration of public courage came at the height of the US military escalation in Vietnam. During the 1966 Christmas season, Bullitt took to the air on KING-TV with a famous editorial that began with an arresting statement:

> *Greetings. Until now I've never broadcast an opinion for this company, but the war and its treatment in the news compel one to speak*

out. The intensity of our military action should be stepped down,
and we should stop bombing North Vietnam.

Dr. Martin Luther King Jr. had not yet spoken out against the war. The Eugene McCarthy and Robert Kennedy insurgencies were more than a year away. Four years later, with Vice President Spiro Agnew berating the media, Bullitt took to the air again, blasting the secret US invasion of Cambodia. The editorials gained him what he considered his greatest honor, a prominent place near the top of President Richard Nixon's "Enemies List."

Stim Bullitt was off climbing Vesper Peak when Nixon became the first American president to resign his office. He refused to gloat when reached at home late that night. "It was not an honor I sought," he said of his presence on Nixon's list.

Stim Bullitt was the second of three children of A. Scott Bullitt, a transplanted Kentuckian, and Dorothy Stimson Bullitt. He idolized his father, who would die suddenly in 1932 while rumored to be in line for a Roosevelt cabinet post. The widowed Dorothy Bullitt would build King Broadcasting from a low-watt AM station in the Smith Tower to one of the city's premier media assets. She was a forbidding if shaping parent.

For Stim Bullitt, proving himself meant escaping from privilege. He worked as a youth in central Washington orchards, and on a highway crew at Chinook Pass. At Yale he became a boxing champion and later won fights in New York City, Connecticut, and Seattle. Why fight? "He wanted to earn everything himself. In the ring, his mother's purse strings meant absolutely nothing," architect Alex Bertulis, a longtime climbing companion, observed.

Fred Nemo, the second oldest of Bullitt's five surviving children, said his father was "very sensitive as a child to privilege. He gave up yachting for boxing. The only [racially] integrated place he could find in Seattle was the boxing ring."

A mastoid infection cut short his life in the ring. "Our mother became worried and called the boxing commission. He learned that and never forgave her," sister Harriet Bullitt recalled.

"Mother gave me to believe that to think well of oneself was wrong," Stim Bullitt wrote. "She condemned conceit as a serious fault and readily discerned it in a modest boast." In his autobiography, he dwells on the areas in which he perceived himself a failure. Of his earlier book *To Be a Politician*, he takes an almost apologetic tone, writing that "this book's deficiencies reflect the limits of my ability, not a failure to use all I had."

Of that book, however, Arthur Schlesinger Jr. wrote: "The brilliant and original book should become a small political classic." Reviewer Richard Rovere described it in the *New Yorker* as "human and humane, funny, hopeful, exciting and ennobling as any civilized work must be." Social scientist David Riesman dubbed Bullitt the "Monsieur Montaigne of Seattle."

Stim Bullitt talked and wrote of self-perceived shortcomings, which often were not shortcomings. He continued—always—to strive. "Because to aim lower seems the coward's or idler's course, I have sought to 'run with the swift': Ski racing with Franz Gabl, climbing with Alex Bertulis, boxing with inner-city Black professionals, practicing with good lawyers, tackling long-sustained business challenges," he wrote.

There were setbacks in Stim's life, to be sure: the acrimonious dissolution of his first marriage, to poet Carolyn Kizer, in the 1950s; the drowning death, in Lake Washington, of his son Ben; the split—healed after two years—with daughter Dorothy over the direction of Harbor Properties.

He made much of his uncomfortable ten-year tenure, from 1961 to 1971, at the helm of King Broadcasting. He was not outgoing, never a schmoozer, and as a man of books uncomfortable with television. "He felt it was intellectually empty and that its influence outran its content," said his son Fred Nemo. Still, he was one of TV's first executives to hire women and African Americans. He started *Seattle* magazine, staffed it with Ivy Leaguers, and watched it scald local institutions from the Downtown Seattle Association to Broadmoor.

Seattle magazine lost money, as did a film division, King Screen. Yet Stim "got us into the cable business early on, when it was affordable, which was brilliant," sister Harriet Bullitt said. A King Screen production, *The Redwoods*, won an Oscar. The TV station helped create the North Cascades National Park with another documentary. It put itself in harm's way with documentaries on the death penalty, urban sprawl gobbling up farmland, and the smears by John Birch Society members and other conservatives that ended the legislative career of State Representative John Goldmark of Okanogan.

Late in life came another achievement. Stim Bullitt envisioned (correctly) Seattle rediscovering in-city living, and created a vibrant micro-neighborhood in the heart of the Emerald City—Harbor Steps, a complex of residential towers adjoining a public plaza and a broad staircase leading from downtown to the waterfront. Upon hearing praise for what he created, Stim would gently reject "the vision thing." How could he *not* have found tenants, Bullitt would ask, with water and mountains on one side and downtown on the other?

Stim Bullitt was an active bachelor through much of his golden years. Bill Sumner, a climbing companion on Mount McKinley, recalled a party scene:

> *One friend had a bit too much wine, and she was on Stim's case about his romantic interests. He was polite and quiet until pushed too far by the remark ,"You seem to enjoy the company of younger women." Stim paused and said, "I enjoy the company of younger men, too." I choked laughing in my beer. The conversation was over.*

Bullitt found happiness late in life with third spouse Tina Hollingsworth, his partner on rock climbs at Joshua Tree and sailing trips to the Mediterranean. The couple would be out climbing by day, then would change out of the car trunk into clothes for a Seattle Opera performance.

Stim was always generous, donating $17.2 million over the years to the Bullitt Foundation, which underwrites environmental causes in the region, and midwifing a family gift of 590 acres for Squak Mountain State Park. He made other quiet gifts, such as the money that allowed James Meredith, the first black student at the University of Mississippi, to later attend law school at Columbia University.

He was a learned, and learning, man until very late in his life. In a letter he once wrote to Jim Wickwire, Bullitt mused about an incident in which

Franklin D. Roosevelt paid a courtesy call to ninety-two-year-old retired Supreme Court justice Oliver Wendell Holmes: "When the president-elect was wheeled in he found the justice in a rocking chair, reading Plato in the original Greek. He asked why. With a smile, Holmes replied, "To improve my mind, Mr. President."

Even as Stim Bullitt faded in the last few years of his life, a conversation with him could be like a snifter of very old cognac. Slowly, when warmed, his memories would emerge, very much like the subtle flavors of a fine liqueur—a rich and wonderful experience.

He would recall, at fourteen, returning from an International Boy Scout Jamboree in Hungary, and traveling with his mother to lunch with Franklin D. Roosevelt at Hyde Park. He would remember the president's booming greeting: "Hello, boys!"

He could be coaxed into what was once the Northwest's funniest mountaineering slide show, chronicling his climb of Mount McKinley with pals Bill Sumner and Shelby Scates. The trio of climbers were pinned down in a days-long snowstorm. Beards grew longer and scruffier. They ripped books into sections so each would have something to read. When nature called, the climbers had to dig through a foot or so of snow to get out of the tent.

Together they waited out the storm, which wreaked havoc on other parties, and reached the summit of North America, where Stim squeezed off a wonderful shot of 17,000-foot Mount Foraker turning purple in the late daylight. But the essence of the experience, and the reason for its success, came in the climbers' exercise of life's unheroic virtues—patience, tolerance, and forbearance.

These were the virtues of Charles Stimson Bullitt. He may not have always appreciated how much he embodied them, but we certainly can.

Joel Connelly
August 2013

Portions of this introduction have been drawn from Joel Connelly's biography of Stimson Bullitt on HistoryLink.org and from Connelly's appreciation of Bullitt's life on SeattlePI.com.

| I |

TO BE A MOUNTAINEER

Climb the mountains and get their good tidings.
Nature's peace will flow into you as sunshine flows into
trees. The winds will blow their own freshness into you,
and the storms their energy, while cares will drop off
like autumn leaves.

—JOHN MUIR, *OUR NATIONAL PARKS* (1901)

MOST WHO BECOME MOUNTAINEERS do so in stages, each one calling for more effort, endurance, or skill than the one before, until they reach the limits of their aptitude or taste. They proceed from hiking and rambling to scrambling; from low summits to remote, high ones; from low angles of climb to steeper ones, perhaps to vertical, maybe even overhanging; from broad, sharply edged holds to thin, rounded ones; from short approaches to long ones; from rough, adhesive surfaces to the smooth and slick; from moderate snow and ice to soft snow and hard ice; from undertakings that extract sweat to those that remove double-digit pounds.

A mountaineer also passes through stages of outlook and role: observer, novice, enthusiast, hobbyist, user, addict, maybe expert. Later, as appetite or capacity wanes, he may pass through some of those stages in reverse.

I never acquired high proficiency as a mountaineer. I had limited aptitude, I took up the sport late in life, and I was attached to my work to an extent that mountaineering could be a diversion for me, but not a total immersion. Yet this has not at all diminished the delight the sport has given me. Mountaineering has been such an important part of my life since passing age forty-five that it has certainly had significant effects; what they are, I'm unsure. Certainly, mountaineering offered me delight, relief, refuge, and consolation. It also helped me keep good health, as I maintained steady outdoor exercise at an age when many athletes sink into sedentary habits.

Even if I came to mountaineering late in life, my exposure to the wilderness began early. As a child I enjoyed playing with other children in the woods near home. When I was in the woods alone, I imagined adventurous scenes. My grandfather told me stories of the Michigan woods in the mid-nineteenth century—stories that involved timber cruising, wolves, campfires, and log cabins in the snow. In one, a man besieged by wolves climbed to the roof, tore off shingles, and threw them down at his enemies.

The summer I turned ten, our family and another took a horseback-riding journey through the central Cascades west and north of Lake Chelan. In an exciting moment, one day my father and I were sitting on a log when a deer walked by, the first I had ever seen. I do not remember seeing other people during this week, although we probably passed someone.

In 1932, a little after Father's death, I hiked with a group up the Dosewallips River in the Olympic Range to the foot of Mount Anderson. Struggling up the trails under my Trapper Nelson packboard, its load including several cans of beans, exhausted me. After a couple of days, when we came upon a steep snowbank, the three boys (including myself) in the excursion took off our clothes and slid down it, dropping off the lip at the foot and landing with a splash in the pool below. We swam to the far side as fast as we could, the water feeling like a hot wire around our necks.

In my childhood and youth, the wilderness was often linked with Indians, who held special fascination. I idealized, romanticized, and sympathized with them. Like German youth, whose watchword has been *Indianer weinen nicht* ("Indians don't cry"), I thought Indians lived enviable, intrepid lives. The Indian was hardy, bold, and brave, forever on the warpath or the hunt; his hallmark was fortitude under pain, whether from toothache or from his captors in an enemy tribe slowly burning him at the stake. Sometimes I would think of him dressed in fringed deerskin pants and moccasins, eyes shaded with one hand, a bow in the other, as he tirelessly glided through the forest on silent, elastic tread.

This picture did not resemble the current multicultural conception of the Native American. Only later did I realize that the wilderness was not a seamless web, that the mountains that constitute a challenging magnet to mountaineers were not a customary haunt for those Native Americans. Yet my early identification of Indians with mountain wilderness, combined with the appeal of each, left me with a lifetime interest in Indians, a curiosity to learn their histories, and a concern with public policy toward them.

Childhood idealizations aside, I did do a little hiking and camping with the Boy Scouts and the family. Once a friend and I hiked from Sol Duc Hot Springs in the Olympics over a pass or two and out along the Hoh River. The second night we slept in a lean-to occupied by two loggers from Forks, who, like us, sought refuge from the hard rain. They were brothers-in-law who so charmed me and enjoyed each other with boisterous vulgarity that I still remember their names.

From ages seventeen to thirty-five, my contacts with the wilderness were slight. I was preoccupied with college, summer jobs, World War II (adjoining jungles had no appeal), law school, law, politics, business, and family.

After returning from the war, I began to work with a desperate intensity. In 1953, I noted: "I stagger along in a vicious circle of working around the clock to keep up with the work, yet continue to fall behind because weariness makes me inefficient." Eventually I sought to break out of this pattern by taking time off for a journey alone in the mountains, "with the flowers in the late spring and early summer." Like many plans, this solo trip did not work out; having produced children, I made my excursions with them, not solo, for about fifteen years, and I never settled into the practice of taking vacations. Most of my mountaineering has been done on long weekends, expanding to several days at a time in rock-climbing areas during old age. But this plan to break my cycle of work did start my journeys into the mountains, and a romance began that has continued for half a century.

The shift from hiking and camping to climbing peaks took place when the children came to prefer activities other than going into the mountains with Daddy. In 1967, when I was forty-eight, I took my first Rainier summit climb, going with a Rainier Mountaineering, Inc. guide service party by the Ingraham Glacier route. On the way up, two-thirds of one crampon broke off, as did the rest of it shortly after starting down. Soon after, the other one came off as we passed above a crevasse. I slipped and began to slide but stopped with the self-arrest method the guide service had previously taught us. This frightened me, as I had little confidence of being held by the tired neophytes adjoining me on the rope. After descent to Paradise, a final annoyance came when I was required to pay for the broken crampons that I had rented.

Nonetheless, I pursued "peak bagging" until the process lost its flavor after doing Washington State's fifty-one highest. I did not undertake technical rock climbing until I was sixty-nine, in 1988, when a climbing gym opened in Seattle. Before that, the only technical climbing I had done was on a low level, what one sometimes confronts on a hike and scramble to a summit.

Some climbers do not have experience with facing fear before they start mountaineering. Since I was taking up mountaineering after a good deal of experience in other aspects of life, I was familiar with trying to face and overcome fear. Being scared was no novelty.

For a long time after getting into mountaineering, my outlook was timid and my practice reckless—not good. A major source of my education was learning from my own mistakes, a poor way to learn anything. When my friend Otto Spoerl and I climbed Mount Hood, a whiteout enveloped us and we had to stop and camp where we stood. Taking turns digging, we made a sunken platform in the snow. We went on and on, trying to level the floor until we found ourselves in a pit with the top of the tent below the level of the slope. To climb in and out, we had to dig a step. The next morning, clear and windless, early climbers from below were startled to see our heads appear on the level of the snow. Spoerl had to drive us home because my eyes were snow-blinded from my failure to protect them during the day of fog. Lesson learned.

When I began serious peak climbing in my late fifties—and ever since—almost all of my companions were far younger and stronger. One evening I was at noted alpinist Al Givler's house with a group planning a McKinley expedition. The guys resembled models for a body-building course, and reminded me of the muscular statue of Leif Erickson at Seattle's Shilshole Marina. I, on the other hand, felt like an elderly page attending the Knights of the Round Table. Still, it was a pleasure to be among my betters.

As I grew in my mountaineering experience, I saw a reduction in my performance anxiety until it transformed into a healthy alertness. A rock climber leading a pitch[1] always feels anxiety when contemplating the next move: *Will I slip on this one? If so, will I bang hard? If my last piece of protection pulls out, will I bang extra hard? Is my belayer awake at the switch?* Once the climber performs the move as he's intended, he has a sense of accomplishment. In comparison, a mountaineer leading on a summit climb feels a more sustained and diffused anxiety: *Should I have turned back half an hour ago? Should I have taken advantage of that good bivouac site? Now there's nothing, and it's getting dark. Should I have made camp before the snow and wind came along and made problems? Am I sure my chosen route is best?*

For all mountaineers, the principal effect of their experience is the cumulative one, the totality. But some episodes, of course, leave a notable impact. One for me was an "epic" on Mount Rainier's Liberty Ridge in early spring of 1979, when I was sixty years old.

On May Day, four of us had set out on the climb. Though none of us had done this route, finding our way was not hard. We seldom faced a choice. At the second uneventful day's end the sky darkened and a storm began, first graupel,[2] rolling down the slope like ball bearings, then a steady fall of wet snow. At 12,900 feet we shoveled a platform into the sharp-edged ridge

1. The distance between belays on a climb.
2. Soft hailstones or wet, hard snowflakes.

and lay down in our bivouac sacks. During the night, three feet of snow fell, wetting our clothes and sleeping bags. The next morning we dug snow and hacked ice until we reached rock, making a cave in which we could roll over but not sit up straight and from which our feet stuck out. My son Ben, my friend Eric, the climb leader, and I occupied it, while Eric's friend Mike, tied to a rope anchored to our six-by-eight-foot platform, went down the side of the ridge a few feet, dug himself a hole, and crept in.

After sixty-two hours the storm abated, then ended, and the sun came out. During this time we lay next to each other, damp from the first night there, and tried to keep from shivering. We were entertained by thundering rumbles of avalanches as they poured over the ice cliffs to our east and west. A few times we heard one coming down upon us from above, where the ridge was broad. As though we were lying on the track before an oncoming train, we could feel the ground trembling beneath us, and we would tremble too. Before reaching us, each avalanche would spill most of its contents over the sides; the rest would pile a load on the porch in front of our cave, covering our feet. One of us would kick loose, wriggle out, shovel off the load of snow, and return to his sack. We lay hoping that the next would not bury us too deep for escape.

Day by day we reduced the portions of food that we consumed until it was all gone. When our stove fuel ran out, we could no longer melt snow, so we ceased to drink. Ben and Eric suffered more from the cold than the other two of us because their down sleeping bags had become sodden. Most of the time we alternately shivered and shoveled.

The immediate cause of our being caught on this icy perch was the storm. In turn, we exposed ourselves to this plight by judgment error and bad luck. At first our concern was slight. During the storm, Ben, age twenty-two at the time, threw a tantrum when he remembered his two tickets to the SuperSonics basketball team playoff game that night. After the first clear day he lost his five-dollar bet with me that a search plane would come by the next day. We were aware that passing time was tilting the odds on survival further against us. After two days of clear weather (a cloud bank below us at 10,000 feet, but sun above) with no one having appeared to look for us, we thought we had been forsaken. As he lay beside me, Ben hit me on the chest a couple of times with his undirected fist, bending his arm at the elbow and saying, "I don't want to die, and I don't want you to die. I love you, Daddy, and I want to spend a lot more years with you."

During our sojourn on the ridge, we conducted ourselves well: no panic, bickering, recriminations, fighting over food, overreactions, or outbursts. Later conversation among us, looking back on this time together, brought out that our dream lives there had been more active than at any time before. Our sleep was fitful and brief, but it churned out dreams. They were not nightmares and they had little plot, but tended to be kaleidoscopic.

We concluded that the risk of succumbing if we stayed put outweighed the avalanche risk of travel on the six feet of new snow. The other three set forth. Weaker than these lads, fearing to slow them too much or to collapse on the snow and freeze that night, I stayed behind, seeing them off with trepidation and hope. I continued to hibernate, conserving energy and heat and enjoying the luxury of lying crosswise in the now-roomy cave, my feet under the roof. My companions sought to pass over the summit and down the easier, standard route, but chest-deep snow turned them back, and they headed down the ridge that we had climbed. We all expected that they would make it out by that night and that the next morning their summoned help would come for me.

I ate my last piece of food, a caramel, and washed it down with the last swallow from my water bottle. All of the next day, the sky was clear above the cloud bank, except for a six-inch snowfall at midday. I kept sticking my head out, searching the sky for help. In late morning, a small plane came in sight, cruising back and forth across the mountain's north side, in a systematic search pattern that indicated my companions had not made it out. If they had, the plane would have known where to go. Presumably, an avalanche had covered them.

From the frozen ledge, I jumped and waved to catch the pilot's eye. Without a sign of recognition, the search plane grew smaller until it disappeared into the blue sky. The plane's departure showed the search abandoned. I guessed I would last no more than a couple of days.

No notion of survival remained, even one fathered by hope, as hope was gone. This awareness did not affect my general beliefs: philosophy, theology, cosmology. My mind did not turn to questions of God, an afterlife, divine punishment or reward, the relation of humankind to the universe. My wits enjoyed none of the concentration that awareness of impending execution is said to induce. I felt only my habitual need to reduce vaporous ruminations to clearly defined thoughts, the only kind that have worth. My reaction was sodden despondency, sullen dejection, a grunted monosyllabic obscenity. No pangs, tears, or sobs, nor even effort to contain them.

Seated on Mike's hard hat, which he had left behind, I wrote two letters. The writing took effort. Weakness augmented the sense that nothing mattered anymore. Of course, in part, it did matter—hence the letters. They comprised two sets of requests to my sister Priscilla, who I knew would carry them out. One concerned items of business, e.g., "My will is in the bottom drawer. . . . Find my wallet in my pants, which are in the back of the car. . . . Turn over to my partner _____ the file on _____." The other one recited farewells to family members and friends, e.g., "Tell _____ that I am proud of him and love him." That done, I could think of nothing more of duty to fulfill or pleasure to seek.

I sat hunched like a glum bump. Late in the afternoon, a sound broke in on my gloomy musings. A plane was heading straight for where I sat. It turned, then dipped its wings as it flew past, then circled back and repeated the signal. This notice that death had been generously postponed provoked a surge of feeling: first, elation at knowing I would live, then grief at the loss of Ben and my buddies (forgetting that only they could have directed the plane to our ledge). I wept over my little boy, down the ridge beneath a load of wet snow. A few hours earlier, thinking my own time was up, I had felt no distress at the others' ill fate.

Before long, an Army helicopter came. In haste, I scooped my gear out of the cave and started to stuff my pack. The rotor blades' blast swept off my sleeping bag and made me drop to my knees to avoid going with it. Unable to land, the helicopter lowered a sack of emergency supplies. As it passed across my porch, I snatched the sack and took out a two-way radio. Eager for marching orders for a liftoff from the chopper hovering nearby, I examined the radio for operating instructions. The only words were a warning that "Any unauthorized use of this constitutes a violation of the Federal Communications Act" and a recital of threatened punishment. Switching on the receiver, I heard: "Holy smoke, we've just blown off some guy in his sleeping bag, over the Willis Wall! We've got to be careful."

To pluck me from the ledge, the helicopter let down a board seat on a slender cable and maneuvered overhead to bring the seat within my reach. I had envisioned taking pictures while hanging on the wire. In the event, however, camera forgotten, I threw on my pack, straddled the board, leaned back, looked up with a grin, and gave a debonair wave, like a pilot about to take off in a World War I movie. I threw both arms around the wire as it whisked me out over the abyss. Under other circumstances, this would have been detestably terrifying, but here the alternative made it easily tolerable. The seat began to spin, reminding me of childhood, when a playground swing would be wound tight and allowed to unwind; on dismounting, the dizzy and nauseated rider would stagger and fall, to the spectators' amusement. My clutch became desperate. Standing over the open hatch, the soldiers cranked in the wire until I was sprawled on the floor like a landed fish.

In a few minutes the helicopter set down on a gravel bar in the Carbon River. Walking down the ramp, I greeted a friend in the Mountain Rescue Council and asked him, "What word of my boy?" He replied, "They made it out." Releasing a sob of relief, I stepped forward into a crowd. After answering a few questions before microphones and TV cameras, I entered my car (parked, by chance, a few yards up the river bank), thinking about how one climbs successfully and uneventfully for years without acclaim, then by one mistake becomes an object of embarrassing attention. When I took off my parka for the first time in six days, the sweater worn beneath it looked as though I had been sleeping with chickens.

After reaching Seattle and helping Ben and Eric settle in adjoining hospital beds for treatment of frostbitten feet (Ben lost part of his toes), I drove to my apartment, turned up the heat, ate heartily from the refrigerator, and went to bed.

During that week on Liberty Ridge, I had felt no loneliness. On survival and return, my awareness of being alive and warm was compelling. After a night's rest I felt fine and went to the office. The experience on Liberty Ridge has affected my outlook ever since, however. In part this came from the inpouring of friends' reactions, expressing their concern at my plight and relief at my survival. This touched and surprised me. I am devoted to a number of friends but, from obtuseness, had felt I was invisible. My brush with fate made me aware of their devotion.

The experience also caused me to savor life, to value it, to remember its uncertainty and realize the worth of trying to make the most of it. In the past, some events (narrow squeaks in the mountains, near misses at intersections) were so sudden and brief that not until afterward did I realize that death had just passed me by. These moments had come and gone without time for thought, were considered only in retrospect, and were soon forgotten. During a few short periods during World War II the surrounding action had made me realize that odds of surviving ranged from fair to poor. But all of us fighting were young, engaged in the most exciting adventure of our lifetimes, and assumed (except for occasional disconcerting moments) that we were immortal.

There was a further effect of Liberty Ridge. For the previous couple of years I had been feeling useless, unneeded professionally or personally, old and over the hill, indifferent to dying. So I had planned to climb Mount McKinley the following month, and to do so solo and by a new route (the toe of the West Buttress—which has since been done by others). The upside opportunity was a score, an achievement, while the downside risk of not surviving was not a minus factor because I did not care; I proceeded with detailed preparations, intensive conditioning efforts, and useless daydreams. Then when the bitter cup of death was offered me, it felt abhorrent. McKinley no longer held the appeal it once had. But I found I didn't despise myself for this, just laughed at myself.

My proximity to so much death in World War II did not leave me with "survivor guilt," but with a substantial and long-sustained sense of "survivor gratitude." I felt a sense of duty to justify those guys' sacrifices, and to enjoy the pleasures in life they'd lost out on. I also felt a sense of duty to make a contribution to the society in which I lived and for which they died. This augmented my ambition toward socially constructive achievement. And the joy to be alive, often felt in the mountains, added to my "survivor gratitude."

The main difference after Liberty Ridge, therefore, was that while I kept on doing the same old things, I enjoyed them even more.

| 2 |

WHY WE CLIMB

Do I long for the simplicity of a climb, to escape from
puzzling and frustrating complexities of my daily life?
Will a good time climbing and camping make me happy?
Am I drawn from within by something that I do not
fully understand?

—STIMSON BULLITT

AT DIFFERENT TIMES MOUNTAINEERING is adventure, opportunity, holiday, escape, search, test, sport, and much more. Only the rarest mountaineer is propelled by a single motive. For most, some factors draw them into the mountains, while others repel or divert to pursuits elsewhere. Some motives both pull and repel, like a fattening dessert. It's worth examining some of the most common motives, so as to better understand the mind of the mountaineer.

DELICIOUS SOLITUDE

Much of one's mountaineering time is spent alone, and for some this is a great incentive. Even when climbing with one or more partners, though you help and depend on each other, cooperate, consult, and signal, for substantial periods you are out of touch, out of reach, often out of sight and sound, and depend on yourself to succeed and survive. Likewise, you largely are alone when hiking up a long trail or snow slope, bent under a load, preoccupied with your breathing and your back.

Partial or complete solitude among mountain beauties is so pleasurable as to draw more than just the antisocial—by which I mean those who detest crowds or humankind. Mountaineering solitude lovers often are comparatively gregarious in town but nonetheless enjoy these periods alone. One delicious feature of solitude in the mountains is the silence. Another is the sense of achievement from going alone.

The writer, chemist, Holocaust survivor, and mountaineer Primo Levi wrote of his climbing buddy Sandro Delmastro that he often liked to climb alone with his "small, yellow mongrel" dog, to which he roped himself. He "set the dog firmly on a rock ledge, and then climbed up; when the rope ended, he pulled it up slowly, and the dog had learned to walk up with his muzzle pointed skywards and his four paws against the nearly vertical wall of rock, moaning softly as though he were dreaming."[3] Some fanatical climbers' girlfriends, along to please, feel like Delmastro's dog. In both circumstances, the lead climber is largely solitary.

For me, roaming the mountains alone offered isolation from the human race (I rarely saw anyone at or near my camps or on the overland rambles, and only a few on the trails). I also savored the sense of independence, the freedom, the control over myself and my actions, and the feeling I could go anywhere and surmount any obstacle in sight. It felt a contrast to the sense of frustration and defeat in the life I left behind, but this awareness did not diminish my pleasure.

Since childhood, I've been a loner. Sometimes my solitary ways are physical, meaning I avoid human association. Other times my solitude has been more psychological, where I may be in the presence of others but am

3. From the short story "Iron" in *The Periodic Table* (1975).

preoccupied rather than communicating. The cause has been predilection, and now it has become habit. My loner tendencies have given me only occasional regret. Except for eleven years I spent away from Seattle and home, my solitude has been cushioned and blessed by the presence of family, friends, and acquaintances.

Despite my having flunked the English courses during all three high school years, reading and writing have consumed much of my time and attention. The pleasure derived from them has been a large motive, but another has been the pleasure from solitude, turning to the pencil and the books to avoid the problems and uncertainties of human intercourse.

For over forty years, I embarked upon solitary mountain ventures. Some of the later ones were more technically difficult because I had acquired the skills to do them. But the early rambles and climbs tended to offer the most exciting adventure, in part because more was novel to me and in part because my ignorance led me into more risk. Alone in the Cascades, Olympics, and Sierras, and on Orizaba, Denali, Rainier, and Hood, I've never been lonely, though often frightened. To describe the sensations of climbing solo, I draw directly from portions of my climbing journal, usually written right after a climb, when the emotions were still swirling in me:

SEPTEMBER 1968. Discouraged with work and business and curious to learn the way to Mount Thomson, which had eluded me in prior scrambles (the Pacific Crest Trail had not yet been put nearby), I hiked from Snoqualmie Pass up the Commonwealth Basin and over and around ridges, avoiding the worst prior errors.

Brush, rocks, heather, talus, and scree. Then up Thomson in a counterclockwise spiral followed by a clockwise spiral. If I had not gone so far and worked so hard to reach this point, fear would have turned me back. My ignorance of the route made the ascent more difficult and hazardous. I would climb over a jutting piece of rock and look down on treetops laced with shreds of mist. Then, on looking backward, I would realize that in climbing zeal I had overlooked the steepening slope until it had become close to vertical. At this point I would feel like a kitten on a telephone pole, wanting to do nothing but hold on tight, shut my eyes, and meow.

From time to time, confronted by ten feet of steep slab to be traversed, where I doubted my boots would hold, I met the problem by backing up a few steps, then running at it, counting on momentum to carry me across. It worked—that is, it did not fail—and the same method was used on other such traverses along the way, met again on descent. This recalls English writer Robert Graves's reminiscence of a cliff in Wales in *Good-Bye to All That*:

> *About fifty feet above the scree—a height that is more frightening than five hundred, because death seems almost as certain and far more immediate—a long, sloping shelf of rock, about the length of an ordinary room, had to be crossed from right to left. This offered no handholds or footholds worth mentioning, and was too steep to stand or kneel on without slipping. It shelved at an angle of, I suppose, forty-five or fifty degrees. One rolled across upright, and trusted in friction as the maintaining force.*

Although the process was similar, Graves was roped to a belaying companion. In contrast to my action, his was not folly.

At the summit at last, silence, a fine view. Anxiety took my appetite for lunch; the platform was so small I again felt something like the kitten, and the prospect of descent made it hard to relax. Back along the same general route, wandering astray here and there. Time, eleven hours. Saw no human all day.

1969. Passed the pond at the foot of Snoqualmie's Red Mountain, left the trail, took the ridge to the northeast, down it over the rocks to the scree below, up to the Lundin summit. The last scramble, with cliffs on each side, scared me. Stayed there only long enough to sign the register; didn't want to delay attending to the disquieting task of descent. Over the Dome, on the way passing and examining the wreckage of a small plane that had smashed into the mountainside. Along the ridge to a crag, thinking it the summit of Mount Snoqualmie. At the top, terrified at the cliffs, was disappointed to find it not a "name" summit where I could sign a register in proof of accomplishment. An anxious descent, then to the north with cliffs above and, more my concern, below. This was the hard way, I learned. A few yards farther to the top of Mount Snoqualmie, ate something, sitting with other climbers. Down easy slopes past Guye Peak, emerging on the Alpental road on which to the car, completing the counterclockwise circuit. Exhilarating though tiring.

STILL 1969. Having planned a solitary climb but depressed and of mixed mind, when early morning came, turned off the alarm clock and did not rise. Later, feeling less worthless and subdued, set forth, more from love of wilderness and action in it and less as a plunge for oblivion through exhaustion (the latter, constant in its presence during those years, though variable in degree). East of Snoqualmie Pass, went up to Joe Lake, along a little-used and rough trail, filled with logs, rocks, roots, overhanging brush, and mud. After consulting compass and map, set off through the woods. Above the timberline, reached the saddle between Huckleberry Mountain and the Chikamin Peak ridge. Along ridges and the grassy edge at the cliff base. Up a chute to the ridge crest, then along it to what appeared to be the castle. Climbed it straight, then discovered that the summit lay beyond. Down the other side along the ridge a few yards to the real castle, where I left my pack. The sides looked as steep or steeper, so proceeded straight, with trepidation, climbing from ledge to ledge up the rock. Since it was late in the afternoon, did not want to consume more time going down and around to look at the far side to see if it might be easier. The knowledge that no one is around to pick you up if you fall makes you concentrate on what you are doing. If I had not invested so much time and effort and reached so close, I would not have made myself go on. Made the Chikamin summit, signed the register, and started down, descending the castle on the easier far side.

Lowered myself past a few sticky spots, then back up to the ridge to collect my pack. A slow, tortuous scramble down a series of chutes, each with a belt of snow running down it and with sides too steep to climb out. The grade on the lower portion of each was out of sight, and some became too steep to down-climb. Thus a series of dilemmas, familiar to many mountaineers: How far to descend the steepening slope before concluding that to descend further at risk was a worse bet than to turn around and laboriously scramble back to the entrance and traverse the upper edge of the cliff to try the next parallel chute?

Down through a wide belt of thick brush, then the rock and gravel bed to its end, along the stream bed, up through the brush to the northwest. Hit upon the trail as the sun set. Hurried down and out. The last hour spent in darkness; the stars were out for the end of this clear day, but the overhanging brush shut out their light. Would have been forced to spend an uncomfortable night in the woods were it not for the good fortune to catch up with two men who had preceded me to the Chikamin summit and who had flashlights. Reached the car at about 9:30. Had been in such a hurry I only stopped to catch my breath and had not eaten the lunch I had brought. Went home tired but satisfied by this and feeling like a man.

1970. Glacier Peak in the North Cascades. After part of the day at the office, drove to the road end and hiked in about 8½ miles, easy grade to Kennedy Hot Springs, then steep to Sitkum Ridge. In the basin, above timberline, darkness fell, and fog came in. Little could be seen close by and nothing at a distance. Lost the trail, staggered and stumbled upward over boulders and shale, looking for a place to lay my head.

Crept along the foot of a short cliff, surmounting it at a dip where water trickled over moss. A light spot on the ground proved to be the label on a bottle, suggesting prior use for rest. A level spot appeared, clear of rocks, the first such spot in 1½ miles and a couple of hours. With gratitude and relief, lay down. In 1867, John Muir, hiking through the Kentucky forests, "lay down in the bushes by guess." When he opened his eyes, "[S]everal beautiful plants, strangers to me, were looking me full in the face. . . . This was one of the most delightful camp grounds, though groped for in the dark, and I lingered about it enjoying its trees and soft lights and music."[4]

4. From *A Thousand-Mile Walk to the Gulf* (1916).

Lay abed next morning, weary from the night, emerged in sunshine to discover the bivouac the best that could have been chosen on this side of the peak: water 20 feet away, heather and wildflowers helped to adorn the foreground where they appeared between the boulders. The high location made a summit climb convenient; no one else was camped within half a mile or in sight. With the stunning view to adorn the scene, I made a leisurely breakfast.

At noon, started upward, leaving flashlight and gear for cold or wet. I intended to go higher to scout the approach to the summit, enjoy the view, find a place to read a book, and find some climbing party to ask to allow me to accompany to the summit next day. A few hundred yards above my bivouac, started up the Lower Sitkum Glacier, which to my ignorant look seemed a big snowfield. At the top of this (where I had intended to sit, read, and look around before descending again), the summit came in sight, evoking the thought, why not give it a go, so proceeded. A short walk over rocks and sand reached the Upper Sitkum, footstep traces followed in the snow, which proved to be a mistake, as they probably had been to the footprints' author. Upward beneath the cliff bordering the glacier, difficulty came in ascending the icefall at the lower end. At one point, chopped a couple of steps in the steep ice and elsewhere kicked footholds with my front points and held onto irregular, dirty ice projections and rocks embedded in the ice.

The upper section of the glacier, on the firm snow surface, was easy walking until at three points along my route, when I plunged my ice ax in the snow, it easily slid to the hilt. Aware of standing on a fragile roof above a dark abyss, I turned around, placed the ax, and again it went all the way; then at each point of the compass until the pattern of holes suggested I was sawing a trapdoor. I sought escape by tiptoeing up the slope, as though to avoid catching the notice of the menacing mountain god.

Climbing a pumice ridge, neglected to look for others' tracks and forthwith climbed toward what I took to be the summit. Up a steep scramble, little of which was severely exposed and almost all of which had plenty of holds but on rock so soft and crumbling that to touch with hand or foot gave the sense that it might drop a boulder in my lap. Finally reached the top, a thin point, held on tight, sought the register, was dismayed to see none, then looked beyond and about 200 yards to the east, at about the same level, saw a stick in a rock formation with a broader top and realized that was "the" summit. Painstakingly descended my crag (which must have been Peak 10,381) and scrambled to the summit, signed the register, and started down.

When danger or much difficulty lies ahead, I can't relax, but want to get the matter over with, partly out of prudence to avoid the risk of oncoming night, but mainly because the prospect denies the pleasure of the moment. Descended on the far easier route, a well-trodden way, and returned to my bivouac. Enjoyed the tranquil evening and lovely sunset. A satisfying day, but realized the risk had been unjustified.

Arose after dawn but before my bivouac saw the sun. Ran out of stove fuel when the bacon and eggs intended for breakfast were half-cooked. No matter, I was content. Proceeded over little ridges to a big one, where enjoyed the splendid view and tried to identify peaks through map and compass. Returned to camp, picked up my pack, and hiked down. At Kennedy Hot Springs, went over to the spring, a square pit about five feet deep, a few yards from the White Chuck River, and took a bath. The bubbles rising along one's body felt like warm soda water (but bigger bubbles), impaired only by the horseflies. Hiked on out, drove back, to the office for a while, a late supper downtown, and home to bed.

1971. In California on business, drove to Carson Pass and hiked north. Snowbanks remained, but the country was open enough to avoid losing the trail. Past Meiss Meadows, wet with swampy ground and many streams from the snow runoff, made camp a little way into the timber; convenient water, plenty of firewood, few bugs, no people. Next day, climbed Red Lake Peak, 10,060 feet, on the ridge. Puffed from the altitude, but it was otherwise an easy climb; short rock scramble at the end. Next day, hiked out. Except for a man fishing in the meadows, saw no one, car to car.

SUMMER OF **1971,** went for five days through the Pasayten Wilderness, northward along the Cascade Crest Trail, with digressions over hill and dale. My stops to read tended to be cut short by the mosquitoes (a late snow year). For the first time on any such trip, I put my watch away and largely escaped bondage to precise attention to time (largely only, since much of the time I was trying to figure out what time it was). This was a successful mountain excursion: simple life, aesthetic and spiritual satisfactions from the beauties of nature, harmony with the wilderness, a sense of permanence, and continuity with the past.

LATE IN THE AFTERNOON AT SUMMER'S END, undertook to climb the Three Queens in the Alpine Lakes Wilderness, starting up the rock in a strong wind. Went the wrong way, tried another, did not know the route, and could not discern one that looked safe, so turned around. Even the point reached was exposed enough to scare me on the descent. On return, had leg cramps. Usually, out in the mountains alone, I felt uncommonly strong, free, and self-sufficient. At times on this occasion, I felt weak, lonely, and, up on the rock, scared. As always when alone in the mountains, however, had a fine time.

JANUARY OF 1981, leaving the car where the Teanaway River road was blocked by snow and ice, ten miles below the trailhead, hiked in and climbed Esmeralda Peak in the Cascades. A few hundred yards east of the summit, reached the summit ridge and followed it to the top. Crampons bit firmly into the well-settled snow. Blue skies and cool; an icy wind on top, but was bundled in comfort. Descended more gentle slopes than on the ascent and traversed eastward beside the peak complex. Just before reaching the road, crossed the river, bordered by brush, sweeping the snow from a slippery log as I inched across it in the darkness above a boiling pool. Strode along in the starlight, enchanted by the silence, down the road to the car and drove home. For the 13½ hours, car to car, the mountains were empty of life, not a soul for many miles.

1983. After a failed attempt on Sharkfin Tower in the North Cascades, tired and sleepy, dozed and drove off the Cascade Pass Road, first one side, bouncing off a tree, and then swerving off the other side before returning to the road. Probably the only place between there and home that one could drive off the road and survive. The only damage was a banged wheel that soon caused a flat. Changed it and drove home.

ON A SUNDAY MORNING, LATER IN 1983, worked at the office for a while, threw my pack into the backseat, and set out for Buck Mountain in the north-central Cascades. From the Trinity Mine, the road end, up the trail, along the Chiwawa River, then Buck Creek. After about 4½ miles, turned off into the brush, crossed the creek, and started up the timbered ridge. When too dark to walk, lay down to sleep on a level spot. A pleasant night under the moon.

Next morning, up the ridge, over it, around a cirque, getting stuck in some brush when I should have gone higher, then along the feet of cliffs and up boulders and scree slopes to a larch-covered ridge between Berge and Buck. Open, easy hiking up over sand, scree, and snow patches to the rock of Buck Mountain. Class 3[5] climbing to the ridge, then along it to the summit rock. The climbing became Class 4, plenty of good holds, though an abyss beneath. Continued until about 20 feet below the top was stopped by prudence and fear, but regarded myself as having climbed this peak.

Retraced my steps, more or less. A seated glissade[6] down a snowfield got out of hand until order was restored by self-arrest. After shaking the snow out of my clothes and finding my wristwatch, which the tumble had torn off, entered the woods under a gently falling rain that barely could be heard. My direction became uncertain when darkness fell as I reached the crest of the wooded ridge, the last obstacle before the trail. Broad and well maintained, it would have been easy to descend in the darkness. Before long the sopping brush had soaked my clothes and pack. Sliding down creek banks, creeping up the far sides, tripping over unseen objects, altering course, became ever more parlous. Made slippery, the rocks, logs, and all else slowed travel. Off course, descended into a valley (intersected by the creek coming down from the cirque) of dense Cascade brush. Spent

5. The Sierra Club System rates terrain from Class 1, hiking, through Class 5, rock climbing.

6. A form of sliding down a slope of firm snow, either crouched and sliding on one's boot soles, or seated with one's heels dug in to moderate one's speed; in both cases, holding the ice ax to one side with both hands as though it were a canoe paddle, as a rudder and a brake.

some time in the dim light, soaked, repeatedly falling, tumbling, rolling, crawling under and over alder and vine maple limbs, in and out of gullies with streams running through them. To prepare for the night meant coming to a stop when the slope underfoot felt not so steep as to need holding on to stay put. Tired, not knowing where things were or which way to go, aware I could not make it out in the dark, groped until reaching a more or less level spot and lay down. Put on my spare clothes and squirmed into the bivy sack. Spent the inordinately long night alternately shivering and trying not to. My sleeping bag held some warmth, even though each move would sound a *squulch*. Impatiently waiting for the day, I began thinking there might be truth in Velikovsky's notion that some concatenation of heavenly bodies had halted the earth for a while (helping Yahweh roll back the Red Sea waters at a critical moment).

At last, gray light filled the sky. Set forth and made it to the trail in an hour and a half. Hiked down, relieved to have left the discomforts and the hazards. In the afternoon, on the way down the Chiwawa River Road, a Chelan County sheriff's car signaled me to stop. A head stuck out the window and a voice said, "Stimson, what have you been up to now?" Pursuant to a concerned call by daughter Dorothy to the sheriff's office, he had been assigned to look; he happened to be a friend of sister Harriet. On the drive back, stopping at a grocery store for a can of cola to keep from dozing off, when I took out what was my last dollar bill from my wallet (presumably sheltered by its place in my pack the previous couple of days) and handed it to the storekeeper, she commented, "Oh, you have wet money." On this excursion, I had eaten four slices of toast, a sliver of cheese, a piece of sausage, and some chocolate squares. On these outings fatigue takes my appetite.

SPRING OF 1984. Seeking to climb Slippery Slab Tower, hiked in from the little spur road. After about the first mile snow appeared, first in patches and eventually almost everywhere. I had planned, as often in the past, to lie down at bedtime. However, when bedtime came, no comfortable spot showed itself, only an expanse of soft, wet snow with a few bare spots at the feet of trees. As time passed, increasing darkness and fatigue made me stumble, slip, wobble, and plunge. At last, at about

11:00, settled on a spot that two hours earlier I would have disdained (an experience often repeated): a rough, down-sloping patch at the foot of a tree with my feet in the snow. Lay down in my bivy sack for a good sleep.

Next day, after a couple of hours up the hill, reached Surprise Lake, still frozen over. On snowshoes, went around to look up the slope below the Tower. Five feet of snow at the lake and deeper above. The soft snow and the slope too steep for snowshoes would make the climb to the crest awkward and hard work. Although the way up could be taken without leaving the woods, which normally offer assurance of safety from an avalanche, risk remained of a soft snow slide that, at least, would bang me into a tree. Went down and out.

RETURNED A FEW WEEKS LATER and climbed the tower, using a self-belaying system that I had devised in my mind during the winter. Errors revealed themselves and had to be corrected (after correction, found it still severely defective). From time to time was scared but made myself go on. The summit register showed this to be the first climb for this year. Saw no one that day except for a couple below the lake on the way down. Felt confident and felt good.

STILL 1984. At the end of the day, left the office and headed south, aiming for Mount Adams, the only place in the Cascades that the Forest Service did not declare an avalanche hazard. All evening the windshield wiper was going. Slept at a motel. Next day, drove until snow blocked the road four or five miles down from its end at Timberline. Walked up the hill for eleven hours, kicking plenty of steps. The weather was mixed: sunshine, overcast, snowfall, thunder, calm and wind. Planned to camp high, to permit making the summit in short order next morning and allow a more leisurely day. Made two dumb mistakes. One was to forget how late in the season it had become, so that the snow was too compact to dig a cave. Between 9:00 and 11:00 in the evening, at about 9,700 feet, I hacked in the ice and icy snow a hole deep enough to provide shelter from the stiff and icy wind. However, no overhang was possible, and the wind blew a steady flow of surface snow, cascading over the lip of my hole, inundating my pack, bivy sack, and everything else. The second mistake was failing to bring matches sure to light, and I could not get my stove going. Steadily colder overall, and my hands getting numb, abruptly packed and walked down in the dark, seeing by the faint light on the snow. At about 9,000 feet, came upon the only other climbers' camp on Adams that day, a man and four teenage boys in two big tents. We had seen each other from time to time during the day. I told him what I had done and how thirsty I was, having been unable to melt snow to parch my thirst. He let me have a quart of water, which I promptly downed. Had hoped that they would invite me to share one of the tents, but they did not, so I lay down between a couple of rocks. My spare clothing that I hoped to add while spending the night was so mixed with snow that it was too cold to put on, so I lay there as is, in my boots. Spent much of the night wiggling to stop shivering.

Next morning too tired and thirsty to go back up, went down, although it was a matchless day for a summit climb: a cloudless sky and cold enough so that one could use crampons without kicking steps. Drove home, so sleepy that I made several stops to park on the shoulder for shut-eye or to drink pop to stay awake.[7]

FALL OF 1988. Sixty-nine years old. I drove alone to Icicle Creek, soloed Jabberwocky Tower, a 5.7 route[8], returned to town, and, in congenial company, attended an excellent performance of the opera *Romeo & Juliet*. Felt, this is the way to live.

SUMMER OF 1996. Seventy-seven years old. A few weeks after doing Mount Hood, a dull though pleasant outing, did Rainier, just for the sake of having done it. John Muir, looking up from his cap, described Rainier as "awful in bulk and majesty, filling all the view like a separate, new-born world."[9] Three slow, dull days. Early on the third, set out from

---

7. A couple of months later I drove down to Mount Adams, climbed it, and reached the summit.

8. The Yosemite Decimal System categorizes terrain according to the techniques and physical difficulties encountered when rock climbing, from 5.0 to 5.15. The ratings from 5.10 to 5.15 are subdivided into a, b, c, and d levels to more precisely state the difficulty.

9. From "An Ascent of Mount Rainier" in *Steep Trails* (1918).

Ingraham Flats, ahead of almost everyone, then came down to Camp Muir in the afternoon about the last. All day people were overtaking and passing me. On the summit approach, the wind blew hard, and on descent, the high temperature made unstable footing.

FALL OF 1998. Seventy-nine years old, set forth again to climb The Tooth. Hiked in, feeling good on a splendid fall day, crisp air, temperature in mid-30s, cloudless sky. An hour up the Snow Lake Trail, another hour contouring westward around the north end of the valley and scrambling up into the rocky basin to the west. Then the bad mistake of going up the north side of the basin too soon. Took this steep, narrow gully to the top of the ridge. The climb was not difficult (Class 4) but it scared me. A few inches of snow covered loose stones and dirt, some frozen, some soft, everything wet and slippery. Even the solid rock on the gully sides tended to be slick with moss. After a little way up I took out the rope, tied one end to the pack, and proceeded without its weight. I was fairly sure by this time that I was in the wrong place but wanted to reach the head of the gully, in part to verify this and in part to find a rappel anchor. Feared that a fall might immobilize me and, not being on the route where anyone knew my intention, I would not be found until next summer. With the rope run out to its full length, the nearest tree still was above me. Under a slight overhang, the pack resisted my efforts—both herculean and precarious—to haul it up the rope while I clung to slippery and undependable holds. Using a sling for a prussic [a type of knot], I untied the rope end from my waist and tied it to the tree, then descended, after scouting the area above and beyond the ridge crest. In the vertical spots this was difficult because the rope was stretched too tight to permit wrapping it around myself in a dulfersitz brake [a way to rappel].

Though clearly, climbing alone has its hazards, it contains the most tranquil silences and sense of peace, the most intense sense of close contact. I made it home from The Tooth, of course, and as all turned out well I felt, again, *this is the way to live.*

KISSING THE WILDERNESS

Mountaineers delight in the wilderness, and some believe the closer the contact they can achieve, the better. The thin, flexible sole of a rock shoe puts you in closer contact with the surface of the mountain than does the stiff sole of a hiking boot, just as riding a motorcycle or bike puts you in closer contact with the road surface and the surroundings than when insulated in a car.

In attractive mountains, you are repeatedly blessed: woods, grass, boulders, waterfalls, heather, snowfields, cliffs of rock and ice, flowers, fallen logs, creeks, chiseled skylines, the passage of the sun, birdsong, shadows, solitude, silence, the texture underfoot, the smells, the magic of the campfire as the sparks fly upward, disappearing in the dark. The blessings come not merely in fine moments but in long stretches of good time. Lounging on a heather bench, you may lift up your eyes to a slanting snow-lined ridge below horizontal scarlet ribbons in the sky. The gentle harmonies of an enchanted evening contrast with the hush of dawn, the early morning light touching the spires above, your lungs filled with high-octane fuel that floats you along, yet lets you keep in touch with the earth beneath your feet, and sometimes your hands, as you discover what lies ahead. Other occasions—as on a stony plateau, in chill, silent moonlight, under a high dome of glinting stars, a stark escarpment rising beyond—infuse you with melancholy.

Famous climber and artist Belmore Browne, mountaineering in the Coast Range peaks of the Inside Passage, noted: "When you stand in a wild country, looking at a jagged line of unknown peaks, cut like steel against the sky, the desire to go to them is well-nigh irresistible."[10] High in an alpine zone, among heather, snow, and rock, you may be carried away by the scene.

"Pure" wilderness—as distinguished from what might be regarded as wilderness only by the proverbial New York tourist—is not the only kind that draws mountaineers. For some climbers, Chamonix in the French Alps is ideal: true alpine climbs with dolce vita. For most alpine climbing, the usual course is an arduous hike up steep grades under a heavy pack, followed

10. From the article "The Country of the Black Sheep" published in *Recreation* magazine (April 1905).

the next day by climbing, after which you return to your wet tent and huddle in it through the night, while your tent flaps and struggles to be released from the stones on which it rests and to sail off on the roaring wind. You melt snow, and heat up something that looks like kitty litter. A companion jiggles you, so some of your dinner spills down your sweater. You wipe your chest and creep out into the snow to attend to your needs. Eventually you make your laborious way over scree and fallen logs, then slog down the trail to your car for the journey back. By contrast, at Chamonix, for a few francs at a ticket booth, you step into a gondola that whisks you up to the alpine wonderland of snowfields, edelweiss, and cliffs. You do your climb and settle back into that gondola, which deposits you near jolly revelry, French food, and a warm, dry bed under a roof.

Whether the ascent happens by a gondola or on foot, there is no denying the sensation at the top that the mountain is sublime. It is quick to remind you lest you forget. Sometimes the mountains show their sublimity by dynamic means of sound and movement: avalanche or storm. On Denali in 1981, at 14,500 feet, the biggest avalanche any of us had observed swept down the face a few hundred yards to the south. The display was huge and scary, but just far enough from us not to harm. Although not the loudest, it was the most awesome and terrifying phenomenon I'd witnessed since the invasion of the Philippines. A great spectacle, it lasted long enough for me to take a series of snapshots. When it reached its nearest point to us, we, standing by our tents, turned our backs, turned up our collars, bent over, braced ourselves for the blast of wind and snow dust propelled upon us, and made an effort to keep our feet. It was sublime.

The delight in wilderness induces in some a missionary zeal to draw others into the mountains. Like those who seek to spread their version of God's word, they want to show the wilderness wonders to others so that they too can enjoy the beauties and the glories.

PLEASURE, PURE AND SIMPLE

What impels many to put out energy in the mountains is not ambition, a seeking for recognition, or even the satisfaction of achievement, but rather the simple pleasure of direct and visible consequences of their actions. Beyond that, it is pure impulse—much like the impulse of the squirrel when put on the running wheel, or the horse that gallops over the meadows on release from the stable after a winter's confinement. In their silence the mountains instill us with an energy as great as does the roar of the crowd in some other sports. Near a summit once, while I was traveling at my usual (in those days) brisk pace, a descending climber asked me, "Say, are you engaged in some sort of race?"

Mountaineering gives pleasures that include the aesthetic and emotional satisfactions from the beauties of nature, harmony with the wilderness, and the sense of permanence and continuity with the past. We know that the mountains will not last forever, that they have been eroding since before our species arrived on this earth, and that our own society now has the means to crack them up, put the chips on trucks, and cast them into the sea. But, compared to the rapidly changing surroundings in which we pass most of our lives, the mountains reassure.

Not least among the many pleasures that draw mountaineers to the mountains is the physical delight derived from the strenuous, and fairly complete, use of one's body. For some, the pleasure comes from adrenaline. Its effects are physical and emotional, and it is as potent a chemical as can be taken in from without. Delight is also taken in the sense of total and continuous absorption in what one is doing, all one's faculties concentrated on a single set of processes. The surroundings enhance this pleasure.

Finally, it must be said that there is nothing that can convey the pure and simple pleasure the mountains bring other than going out and climbing them. The difference between looking at the mountains and climbing them resembles the difference between looking at a picture and painting one, or between attending a concert and performing one.

LOST AND FOUND

When you are climbing mountains, the world is not too much with you, or with you at all, because you are removed from your main world. Mountaineering thus speaks to an impulse to escape from the safety, monotony, artificiality, and comfort of modern urban life. British writer and historian Alexander William Kinglake, in his 1844 book *Eothen: Or, Traces of Travel Brought Home from the East*, wrote of how there comes to a young Englishman "a time for not liking tamed people—a time for not sitting in pews. . . . [Y]ou find yourself bending your way to the dark sides of her mountains—climbing the dizzy crags—exulting in the fellowship of mists and clouds, and watching the storms how they gather."

As I mentioned earlier, a few are drawn to mountaineering for self-realization—a sense that they may find themselves in the mountains. Mountaineering may represent a search for enlightenment, for self, maybe for salvation, for the secret meaning of life, or for moral or spiritual achievement or condition, like John Bunyan's Pilgrim in his progress to the Delectable Mountains[11] or Dante's effort to reach Paradise by climbing Mount Purgatorio.[12] American mountaineer Willi Unsoeld found that wilderness experience was religious experience. I do not understand this, nor have I any notion what proportion of mountaineers this motive may pull. For example, bouldering (unprotected movement over outcrops) never has taken me to the "kinesthetic awareness" reached by some. It reminds me only of having sliced some knee tendons in falling off an overhang because I couldn't remember the sequence of holds I'd followed to get where I was.

OBSESSION

Among mountaineers, obsession tends to be a seething, brooding preoccupation with a route or peak, and obsession flows from failure. Reliving the frustration, an obsessed mountaineer can think of little else and burns to try again. Success evaporates the obsession. I never have known of a mountaineer obsessed by a mountain on which he had succeeded, whether he felt vindicated, permitted, or blessed.

11. From Bunyan's allegory *The Pilgrim's Progress*.
12. From Dante's allegory *Purgatorio*, the second part of *The Divine Comedy*.

People have criticized, or commented on, me as obsessed. I admit to becoming "absorbed" in various activities. As to mountaineering, the critics may make something of two habitual practices. For one, although I've rarely been much more than a weekend mountaineer, I've admittedly been frustrated by defeat on a summit or a route, brooding and daydreaming over future tries, planning them and repeatedly trying again. These temporary obsessions, if one insists on that term, have come often. I have not focused on the physical conditions that defeated the venture, nor have I directed the blame or credit on my companion for that climb. I simply feel thwarted by the failure, whatever the causes, and by my own limitations of capacity or nerve. My thoughts have not been angry or resentful, but they have been consuming, expressed by repeated tries, often taking a long drive and hike, then looking up and backing off at the foot of the route. This has worn the patience of friends, one by one dragged along as partners, who have had to share our wasted journey, frustrated by my loss of nerve. Sometimes an obsession would last for more than a year, until I either made the climb or resigned myself that it was not to be done. After such a moment, the subject would drop from my mind.

Outer Space, in Leavenworth, took six tries, and I finally accomplished the climb with my friend Monique Dedinas in the summer of '92. To solo the Overexposure route on Liberty Bell in the North Cascades took three tries and innumerable brooding daydreams before it was put away. To lead Lightning Crack in the Peshastin Pinnacles between Wenatchee and Leavenworth took seven tries, done at last in the summer of 1995 at the age of seventy-six. One short section of a hand jam crack baffled me. Iguanarama, an overhung 5.10a, outside Seattle, took only a few tries but countless visits. On each of these routes I fell at least once. I would drive out alone, hike in to the cliff, and then merely study the route, sometimes with binoculars, sometimes clambering up as far as the second bolt, trying to figure the right moves. A good quantity of time was spent move-by-move on Yosemite's Royal Arches. I had not been defeated on this one but had climbed it as second, and wished to lead it. Denali took three tries and Rainier over a dozen for four successful routes, but somehow these did not provoke daydreams, except for a short period in 1979 when I daydreamed of soloing Denali by a new route. A few weeks later, the near miss on Liberty Ridge in Mount Rainier cauterized that insanity from my mind.

Some of those obsessed are drawn to make one summit after another, one first ascent after another. Among those who are so afflicted, absorbed, or drawn (depending on how one sees this condition), the principal driving force is often competitiveness. For example, if you go off to a distant place to seek a first ascent with world-renowned climber Fred Beckey, the most driven mountaineer I have known, you and he will have crossed the border into the other country before he will reveal the name and location of the climb. The target is kept secret until then for fear someone else will learn the plan and get there first. French climber Maurice Herzog, referring to noted mountaineer H. W. "Bill" Tilman, said, "Climbers always like to keep their plans dark beforehand."[13] Most of us are not so narrowly absorbed for all of our lives. Those who tend to become obsessed, be it with stamp collecting, horseback riding, the saxophone, or the Beatles, are so preoccupied for only a limited period. Beckey is one of those singular humans who has been absorbed in a single interest for a long lifetime.

ADDICTION

In contrast with obsession, mountaineering *addiction* is a compulsion to return to the mountains, and to return with pleasure. Some mountaineers show classic addictive behavior. To quote Tom Hornbein, this behavior includes "[c]ompulsive desire, loss of ability to control the dose, and persisting despite adverse consequences to themselves and others." On the whole, the happiest addicts I've ever known have been mountaineering addicts. The spiritual searchers are outnumbered by those whom this irresistible compulsion drives onward. Willi Unsoeld—who, like Hornbein, was part of the first American expedition to summit Mount Everest—named a son Krag (after a mountain in Canada) and a daughter Nanda Devi (after a mountain in India). Well-known climber Eric Bjornstad displayed this concentrated

13. From *Annapurna: The Epic Account of a Himalayan Conquest and Its Harrowing Aftermath* (1997).

focus on his chosen recreation when he named his son Eiger (in the Swiss Alps), his daughter Heather (after a mountain in Canada), and his rabbit Piton (from the Caribbean volcano of that name).

Addicts are surrendered to their habit. Fred Beckey, expressing his ardor for a woman, named a rock spire after her. He named the rest of the spires along the ridge after each of her favorite drinks. Now they are known as the Wine Spires (Burgundy, Chablis, Chianti, Pernod).

I have displayed some compulsive behavior myself, I suppose, though I wouldn't categorize myself as an addict. During one journey, I went off route on Leavenworth's Snow Creek Wall. I feared falling, then looked up at the blue sky and fluffy clouds and thought, *How enchanting it would be to sit in the cockpit of a sailboat on the Sound*. Then came a slip, a smashed ankle, and a long, long day. Back in town, on crutches at age seventy-two, I started shopping for a sailboat, bought one in the Mediterranean, named it the *Outer Space* (after the fallen-from route), and sailed it across the Atlantic. After ten years of sailing it on Puget Sound and thereabouts, while continuing to climb, I sold it. This reflected neither disappointment with sailing nor addiction to mountaineering. It simply expressed the greater pleasure the mountains gave than did the sea, as well as the discovery that my body had not yet ceased to let me climb.

COMPETITION

For some an incentive to climb is competition, whether with others or with oneself. Summits may substitute for lack of success elsewhere. Desire for approval, from peers and fans, adds to the draw. In *Stones of Silence*, conservationist George B. Schaller's book about the Himalayas, he writes: "There is something uniquely egotistical in scaling summits. Peaks are not climbed anonymously; success is not nurtured as a private joy. Few climbers follow Emerson's personal dictate: 'My life is for itself and not for a spectacle.'"[14]

Competition among mountaineers takes different forms. For some trophy hunters, summits measure success in the way that some other men keep count of their one-night stands. Famed British critic John Ruskin

14. From "Self-Reliance" in *Essays: First Series* (1847).

wrote of Alpine climbers: "[W]ith less cause it excites more vanity than any other athletic skill. . . . You have made racecourses of the cathedrals of the earth."[15] Ruskin's disapproving view is sound if peak bagging is one's exclusive motive. Other ambitious mountaineers take a more sophisticated approach, choosing summits because of their difficulty and infrequency of attainment.

An aspect of ambition is earning acclaim, and to do so many climbers supplement their achievements by advertising them. The longing for fame leads a few to falsify their achievements, as did American explorer Frederick Cook, who claimed, apparently falsely, that he had climbed Mount McKinley and reached the North Pole, when none before him had done so. They substitute a made-up story for the real thing, which has eluded them. Much like those who fabricate their war experience, sometimes boasting climbers come to half-believe their stories. Some are driven to fraud from anger that a rival had achieved the goal.

One of my favorite mountaineering stories illustrates how tempting it can be to veer from truth. One evening in the Chilliwacks in British Columbia, Seattle litigator and climber Jim Frush and his partner were resting in their bivouac on the Redoubt summit when, below them on the North Face, they heard voices discussing whether to continue upward on this difficult route or to give up and retreat. A voice floated upward, "We're close to the summit; why don't we go down and say we made it? No one will know."

At this proposed omission, a deep voice from above boomed in the darkness: "God will know." Thereafter, silence reigned, and the pair remained alone.

Though competition has never led me to be dishonest, I do have a very competitive nature. I sometimes wonder why I became competitive in my late twenties, when I had not been so before. In school, I never competed for grades. I took part in competitive sports, but the motives were pleasure and to be manly. Winning did not seem so important (although in boxing, for obvious reasons, my reaction to winning and losing was strong).

Though I have never come to a conclusion as to my own competitive nature, I have enjoyed studying the natures of other competitive men and

15. From the preface to *Sesame and Lilies* (1865).

women. Jim Wickwire, a notable Seattle climber, wrote a book (coauthored with my daughter Dorothy) about his life and climbing adventures titled *Addicted to Danger*. A more accurate (though less dramatic and succinct) title might have been *Addicted to Competition While Confronting Complex Moral Choices*. The scope of Wickwire's book goes much further than the mountains, and concerns moral decisions in a life of action, thought, and risk. (Indeed, one who would call this a "mountaineering action tale" would call Joseph Conrad's novels "sea stories.")

Wickwire found himself gifted as a climber and pursued his high-stakes avocation to the summit of the mountaineers' austere band. He is a man without habitual introspection or a philosophic bent, yet possessed of strong principles. As such, he struggled with the issues that his life put before him. As with most of us, the issues sometimes won. Some concerned his duties to his family, others his responsibility to his law partners. He neglected them and put them, through himself, at risk. Yet his personal conduct did them honor, and as to economic results, he delivered the goods.

His inner conflicts of principle often were intensified by reminders of the tightrope he trod. In one harrowing and spectacular episode after another, a friend climbing beside him fell to his or her doom. Yet this singular package of character, body, and mind was no more addicted to danger than Michael Jordan was addicted to hotels, planes, and offensive autograph seekers. With both men, competition was the irresistible drug. The rest (danger, planes, and hotels) was merely part of the accepted price. Wickwire does not drive with an unbuckled seatbelt.

I understand Wickwire's competitive nature, and the nature of mountaineers like him who seek first ascents and new routes. Although these are not a high priority for me, I have enjoyed trying and sometimes succeeding at such goals. In 1985, when I was sixty-six, I went to northern British Columbia, east of Wrangell, Alaska, with Fred Beckey and his accomplished climbing partner Alex Bertulis. A chopper landed us at about 6,100 feet on an unnamed ice cap. On a windless, cloudless day, with hard snow underfoot, we headed up the nearby glacier and climbed Mount Pattullo by a couloir and summit ridge, then traversed the mountain, going down first on a short face and then a long ridge. We did not linger on the 8,955-foot summit or even gather there together because a cold wind blew. The space was small, and the snow was corniced, so we passed over the top, one by one, and kept on our way. We used crampons and ice axes and were roped, but did not belay each other except for moments when crevasses were crossed. After return to the ice cap—on snowshoes because by then the snow had softened—we set out over an ice pass, on a glacier traverse of some of Pattullo's twenty-six glaciers, and down into a valley on the other side. We stopped to bivouac about midnight, surrounded by a stark beauty of snow, ice, and rock. According to Beckey, no one had ever trod this area before us.

The next day we proceeded up and down hills, crossing ice fields and ice caps, down a glacier into a valley, at last off the snow and into the woods. The only hazard point in our journey took place in the crossing of a turbulent stream. Alex and I watched with absorbed amusement as Beckey fought the overhung snowbank to climb out of the icy creek.

Eventually we reached an abandoned mining road, which we followed through woods and brush about seven miles to the highway. We hitchhiked thirty miles to the haunts of men. In the forest, we were put on the alert when we came upon the fresh tracks of two bears, one set the size of dinner plates, the other the size of butter plates. We devised our cunning plan to meet this prospect. One of us kept in hand our fuel bottle; another held matches. If confronted by the makers of the tracks, we would pour the gas around us and ignite it so we could stand, defiant and safe, in a circle of fire. Our strategy was not tested.

In 1987, Beckey, Bertulis, and I sought to make the first ascent of Mount Styx, near Bella Coola in the British Columbia Coast Range. First we drove forty miles up an abandoned logging road. The Noieck River, barring our way to the mountain, was too deep and swift to risk trying to ford. We hiked along it for half a mile, then inflated a rubber boat that a local man had lent us. Here the slow-flowing river had expanded to a small lake. The next morning, I took several trips to ferry our gear and party members across to the far bank, where we left the boat and proceeded down the river bottom, then up the side of Mount Styx. We traveled through a short band of thorny brush, after which came a long stretch of easy hiking up a timbered, moss-covered slope into which steps were easy to kick. We ventured out on slabby rock, interlaced with frequent streams flowing from the glacier above. Then came a stretch of brushy cliffs—Class 4 climbing that we did unroped, to my anxiety and discomfort—then lower-angled slabs above. We camped on heather that covered a ridge overlooking the glacier below the summit. We were lucky; this was the only suitable camp spot we had come upon since leaving our camp the night before.

Rain started to fall at about midnight. By morning, we and all we had were wet, and we were socked in. Unable to try for the summit, we headed down. We couldn't see far, and had trouble finding the spot where we had come up the brushy cliffs. When Beckey located it, we went down by several rappels. After that, though not dangerous or arduous, the going was slippery. Several times we slipped and fell. The boat had lost some of its air and the bellows would not work, so our return took place with narrow freeboard, and with relief we finished our journeys across this lake into which, from time to time, the glacier dropped little icebergs. We hiked down the river bottom to the road and with stove fuel got a fire going that partly dried our soaked clothes and sleeping bags.

We returned the following summer, this time having a chopper set us down on the ridge close to the point where we had turned around the year before. Bertulis and I reconnoitered the route on the lower section of the glacier. Beckey and I slept in my tent set on the snow, and Bertulis nearby in an angle of the rock. The next day, we went up the glacier. The going was easy at first, then more complex—up, over, and around crevasses and blocks. The crux came at the 'schrund[16], over a short overhang of ice in an awkward spot. Then came a long climb of forty-five-degree snow, most of it in a series of couloirs. At the top, we encountered a short stretch of easy rock. Lovely sunshine graced our trip all the way, and from the summit we could see much and far. The route we took was the only feasible one. During our descent, the weather came in and rain started. In the lower part of the glacier, we raced. The chopper picked us up moments before the weather would have turned it away. If so, we might have been stuck there for a week. This

---

16. *Crux* means the hardest part; *'schrund* is short for *bergschrund*, a deep and often broad crevasse or series of such crevasses, frequently occurring near the head of a mountain glacier.

climb's degree of difficulty was about right, and satisfied a competitive need. If it had been a pushover, the first ascent would have given little satisfaction. On the other hand, a desperate experience that left one with nightmares and gratitude for survival might have been excessive.

In many sports, people assign a big space between a win and a close loss. As they used to say when I was an amateur boxer, "If you fight a hard and gallant fight and lose by a narrow margin, the crowd will stand and applaud you when you leave the ring, but next week they'll go watch the other fellow fight." So it is in climbing. When I returned from Alaska after fighting storms on Denali but turned back near the summit, I was given a ride home from the airport on the baggage in the back of the Wickwires' station wagon. A year later, on return from having made the last couple of hundred feet, we three climbers were met by TV cameras and microphones.

Not all mountaineers put an emotional competitive gulf between the top and not quite, however. Friends of mine, a married couple, he a leading mountaineer of his day, undertook a climb together, deep in the Cascades. They stopped to rest when they were a couple of hundred feet from the summit. After a while, the wife, tired but fully able to proceed, urged her husband to finish the climb while she took her ease before their descent. He found her choice most difficult to understand. It is safe to assume she did not share her husband's competitive drive, but that is not to say she enjoyed her day any less.

PROVING MANLINESS

Some men take mountaineering risks to prove their manhood, whether to others or to themselves. (If this has a counterpart among female mountaineers, it may be a competitive aim to equal male performance.) Some young men undertake mountaineering under the illusion that the glamorous label of "mountaineer" will help them attract the favor of girls. But they may discover in time that wives and lovers of intense climbers, wracked by loneliness and anxiety, love them not *because* but *despite*.

For me, to be a man, whatever that is, has been a lifelong wish/motive/aim. In its pursuit, I've oscillated between recklessness and timidity. With a few exceptions, my risk-taking choices did not depend on the presence or absence of others. In fact, my biggest risks were taken alone.

Not until after I became a climber did I read Ernest Hemingway's declaration that the only sports for "real men" (he didn't use quotes) were bullfighting, motor-racing, and mountaineering.[17] Nor had I read Robert Graves's opinion that "the sport [climbing] made all others seem trivial."[18] So these words had no effect on the course I took. I have no bullfighting experience, so cannot compare it to rock climbing. Boxing, if undertaken seriously, exposes one to certain exhaustion and risk of humiliation, injury, and pain in return for the possibility of self-satisfaction or others' recognition for manly qualities. Several years' experience as an amateur boxer let me know Hemingway was right. His judgment on rock climbing was true when he wrote it, but no longer. Safety improvements have transformed the sport from extreme hazard to one that can be done at modest risk, in a way that is quite dangerous only by negligence or by choice.

A few times in my late seventies I undertook a solo summit climb and then, a short way up the trail, gave up and turned back. I wondered why I'd gone out in the first place. What was the matter with me? Was I trying to prove manhood? If so, did it matter? On past occasions my behavior had offered reasonable proof of my manliness. Why wasn't I convinced? Was further repetition required? And if, near eighty, proof had not been displayed, was it not too late to achieve? Was I yielding to a competitive urge, giving myself another score to put down on my list of major climbs, posted on my library/study wall beside a list of published work? To acknowledge that I was devoting days, energy, and risk to a secret satisfaction in an insignificant achievement suggests an outlook on life so immature that awareness of it should inspire not pride but shame. I would go home discouraged and upset, wondering if I had recovered my senses or lost my nerve. My mind told me the former, my feelings the latter. I would feel craven, disgusted by my irresolution, even with the wasted time. Soon, however, I would recover. I would start dreaming of a new expedition to my beloved mountains.

17. This quotation is often attributed to Ernest Hemingway, but the exact source is uncertain.
18. From *Good-bye to All That: An Autobiography* (1929).

| 3 |

A MOUNTAINEER'S COMPANION

One tribute to his twenty-year experiment in the human dynamics of mountaineering is that he has never lost a partner.

—Greg Child, writing about Polish climber Voytek Kurtyka in *Mixed Emotions*

Perhaps more than any other mountaineering practice, choosing one's partners with care improves one's odds: for pleasure, safety, and success. No choice deserves more weight than the choice of one's companions. They affect one's risk by their nature and quality, their efforts, and their errors. This applies to the decision to undertake a climb, followed by the string of decisions made either jointly with one's companions or by one of them with consequences that affect the rest. Good selection—whether by judgment or by fortune—can better one's odds across the spectrum, improving the prospects of success and reducing the odds of harm. Pete Boardman, the British mountaineer lost on Everest, wrote in *The Shining Mountain* that committing one's weight to a rope after someone else has anchored it resembles "the jester sampling the king's food for poison."

For safety, one does well to confine one's climbing companions to those who make conscious moral choices according to principles one shares. These principles may have their source in some institutional religion that supplements its faith with doctrines and rules of conduct. Or they may be derived from a rational outlook drawn from one's upbringing, respect for tradition, and others' examples.

Two kinds of mountaineering companions should be avoided. One is a subscriber to a religion or philosophy that is so muddled and vague that no principles of conduct may be derived from it—someone with a "feel good" approach to the conduct of life, who treats impulse as a theological license for self-indulgence.

The other kind of companion to avoid is one indifferent to preserving life. One afternoon I was traversing a steep hillside with a stranger I'd met through a bulletin board. The footing was easy but precarious—wet grass, heather, and mud. We had been trying to climb Mount Garfield in the Cascades but had not found the route and by then had lost our way in rain and mist. The creek in the gully below us was covered with snow, except for a hole directly beneath us. Uneasy at the prospect of falling through it and being taken under the snow roof, as if swept into a sewer pipe, I remarked, "That'd be a hell of a way to go." He replied, "It doesn't matter how you go; all that matters is whether you're ready to meet your Maker." To which my unspoken response was "Not ready to meet mine, I wish not to climb with one who is so prepared."

Once I climbed a fine ten-pitch rock route with a guy I'd not met before. Experienced, young, and strong, he led. Over the course of the climb he fell once, a piece of protection dropped from his placement, he dropped a quickdraw off the cliff, and his gear sling came unbuckled (fortunately, not until we had started our rappels) so that the rest of his gear sailed off into space. Several times while I was climbing and within his sight, I had to remind him to take up the accumulating slack ("up rope"). He gave me none of the advice I had requested. This and more was disconcerting.

I recall another time when a partner's behavior gave me trouble or anxiety. By fingers and toes I was clinging to the East Face of Chair Peak, near Alpental, and looked down between my legs to see, to my alarm, that my young companion, impatient at my slow pace, had ceased to belay me and had resumed his climbing.

I'm not sure I've always been a desirable companion myself. I once awoke from a dream in which I'd been kicking in anger at a dog snapping at my ankle. When I opened my eyes, I was on the Emmons Glacier in Rainier and discovered I had been kicking my companion, Rod Brown. When morning came, we cancelled our climb of Rainier and headed down, attributing our decision to the avalanches heard roaring down above us on that hot July night. I was left wondering if, despite his effusive assurances that he took no offense, Brown had concluded he had made a judgment error in his choice of a climbing partner.

A stronger memory of shame—for an action that imposed both discomfort and insult—looks back to 1984, when five of us set out to climb Rainier by the Tahoma Glacier route. At 9,100 feet, I shared a tent with celebrated climber Jim Wickwire and Peter Jackson, Senator Scoop Jackson's son. On reaching 11,000 feet, we turned around. A heat wave had made the snow so soft that on the steepest stretches one's footing risked breaking loose. The risk would have been aggravated by returning late in the afternoon, with the snow even softer and the two inexperienced members tired. On the way down, ahead of the other four, I decided to gallop down so I could await the others while reading in the car. Below Tokaloo Spire, I turned left when I should have turned right, and soon was lost and meandered for hours in a rapid hustle up one ridge and down the other, searching for the way out, wishing to avoid delaying my companions and then to avoid the risk of embarrassment if I did not show up for a day or two. At last, after coming upon my party's footprints in the snow above St. Andrews Park, I looked for a companion who the ranger on the trail said was staying behind to wait for me. Seeing no one among the parked cars and figuring they had gone home, I gloomily trudged down the road toward the park entrance twelve miles off, until my thumb got me a ride. Alas, the next morning I discovered that Jim Wickwire, the leader, had stayed there overnight, looking for me. I had forgotten the strong unwritten rule that one does not leave the mountain until sure that one's companion does not need help. It was hard to face him when I picked up my clothes, containing wallet and keys, at the Wickwires' front door.

In smart, short expeditions, incompatibility rarely occurs, and if it does, it can be addressed at little cost by canceling or by remembering not to repeat one's choice. But in big, long expeditions, the risk of friction among ambitious, hard-driving egotists is high. To assemble a group that will not come apart in acrimony followed by blame, those who recruit and those who enlist must take extreme care. Concentration is harder to maintain when holding your temper.

Regardless of an expedition's length, whether a day or three months, and regardless of a party's size, not only should each be congenial with all, but the range of capacity should be narrow. A spread does not necessarily cause acrimony or even friction, but it impairs pleasure, effectiveness, and success. The stronger, in their hunger for the goal, are held back in impatience and frustration, while the weaker struggle to keep up in exhaustion and embarrassment and sometimes are neglected, to their harm.

Your climbing companions should also be people you enjoy. You need to select them carefully not only for safety and reliability but for your pleasure. When Alex Bertulis and I were hiking in to the Chilliwacks from the Canadian side, he noticed me struggling to maintain the pace. He stopped and said he was having trouble keeping his pack in balance, and requested some of my load to equalize his. This gracious tact gave me almost as much pleasure as the lightening of my load. And as we were coming down from the summit of Formidable, after making a new route on its east side, I, with firm confidence, declared that the best way was where I pointed. He politely disagreed, and we separated, each to his own. When I finally caught up with him where he waited at the start of the trail, he did not gloat. Several times I have become separated from companions and gotten lost, and on our eventual rejoinder I've been grateful not to be scolded or even unduly teased.

As to partners of another kind, attached couples often mountaineer together, but romance rarely starts in the mountains. When it does, it can be harmless, as when men fell for Seattle-area climber Marty Hoey in the mountains of at least three continents. But romance that starts on an expedition may disrupt the group, as with one expedition I knew of on which an extra-marital affair took place between a married woman and another member of the party. As it happened, the woman's husband was also a member of the team.

I can recall a companion being angry with me only once, and it did not involve an ethical issue. It occurred one night on descent from a summit. My somersault from a stumble had broken one of my ribs. A deep breath hurt, as did a cough or laugh. My mood was not genial. Sharing my tent was an ill-tempered female climber. A blizzard in full tilt made an excursion from the tent unappealing, so I relieved myself in a plastic bottle. She sought to do the same, with spillage over herself and her sleeping bag. In frustration at the result and anger at my amused smile, she flung the (remaining) contents in my face. A stab of pain was probably deserved punishment for my heart-less reaction to her chagrin—not anger, but a guffaw.

COMRADESHIP

Companions in the mountains may become comrades. And comradeship may develop into deep and gratifying friendships, just as shared values and experience do in other walks of life. Like other sports, mountaineer-ing does not limit the scope of your kinds of friends, though it limits your opportunities to make friends with other interests. On the whole, friendships made in mountaineering are more an unexpected reward than a motivating incentive.

The ties and tone of these relationships vary: easy humor; strictly busi-ness; enduring affection and pleasure in companionship. Of course, some-times it works the other way: passionate acrimony followed by sullen rancor; interactions cool, guarded, and laconic; or conversations no further from the day's task than general shoptalk.

A distant formality marked the congenial climbing British pair of Eric Shipton and Bill Tilman. Even after years of interdependence in Himalayan fastnesses, Tilman never addressed his friend by his given name. Characterized by reserve, Tilman wrote in *The Ascent of Nanda Devi* that at the moment he and fellow British climber Noel Odell attained the summit (first ascent, yet) of Nanda Devi, "[W]e so far forgot ourselves as to shake hands on it."

Less reserve was displayed by the Parker-Browne party in 1912 after their near miss for the first ascent of Denali. When they reached their base camp on the tundra after being away for twice the forecast absence, Belmore Browne reported in his diary that their companion, still there to their relief, "came to us, tears of happiness running down his cheeks, and we forgot our stiff-necked ancestry and threw our arms around each other in a wild embrace, while over us, under us, and all around us surged an avalanche of wooly dogs."[19]

Writing in the mid-nineteenth century of a journey through Palestine, Alexander William Kinglake referred to his paid helpers in *Eothen*: "I always liked them, but never perhaps so much as when they were thus grouped together under the light of the bivouac fire. I felt towards them as my comrades, rather than as my servants, and took delight in breaking bread with them, and merrily passing the cup."

One's friends can enhance one's mountaineering experience, or they can have an opposite effect: nerves may be rubbed raw. The most congenial companions with the most adjustable personalities nonetheless may suffer frayed nerves after weeks of stormbound captivity in a tent or cave. Rivals compete for distinction. On big expeditions to big mountains, frictions develop. These range from cooling friendships to estrangements to fierce enmities that may endure through long-nurtured feuds. A common situation is when a collection of all-stars accustomed to having their way are put under a leader whose authority is weak. Each of these ambitious climbers wants to make the treasured summit by the treasured route. Each envies and resents those named for the first (and possibly only) try. Each resents the leader who assigned them. Concerning recriminations over the disastrous 1939 American K2 party (failure, plus four deaths), mountaineer and author Jim Curran wrote: "[T]he arguments were compounded by guilt, sorrow, revenge and ignorance."

A poignant form of comradeship was displayed between Jim Wickwire and Seattle's young climber Chris Kerrebrock, deep in the dark crevasse

---

19. From *The Conquest of Mount McKinley* (1913).

into which they had fallen at the foot of the Wickersham Wall on Denali. Chris, wedged in the ice too tight to be extracted by Jim's most extreme exertions, was freezing to death. Like Radamés and Aida in the tomb,[20] they exchanged affectionate farewells.

A comrade's personal idiosyncrasies, if they do not interfere unduly with functions at hand, may add more entertainment than they subtract in convenience. Years ago, a law partner friend and I, with his female companion, climbed the south ridge of Ingalls Peak. At the top, my friend wanted to memorialize the triumph with a photograph. His companion, to be helpful, took his camera from his pack, but dropped it as she handed it to him. We watched it sail downward to be shattered below. It seemed that the relationship between the two had not been irreparably severed by *l'affaire camera*, however. The following morning, I left our tent (which my friend had insisted be placed in a spot that was so tilted that the night was spent with us three sliding to the lower edge) but returned soon after, seeking refuge from the fog and chill wind. My knock for entrance was greeted by the zipper opening a few inches to disclose my friend's broad grin. His voice decisively said, "We're resting," and I was left to swing my arms on a patch of snow and hope for the sun to come out. Since then many years have passed, and we have embarked on many more undertakings together.

It's worth noting that two people on the same path can have entirely different perceptions of it for reasons as basic as their choice of footwear. In the summer of 1969, my son Ben and I completed the circumambulation of Rainier, much of the time in the rain. As we approached Longmire, I hurried ahead to try to get us a room at the inn. He took a wrong turn, so did not arrive. I went off to look for him, then ran back and found him in the lobby, his eyes filled with tears. For him, the day's toil had been hard. Having outgrown his hiking boots over the past couple of months, he was wearing tennis shoes. (He was not so far gone, however, that he had been unable to obtain from the desk clerk a key to a room with a bathtub.) The total circuit was about ninety-five miles. I had imagined this route to resemble hiking

20. In the final act of Verdi's *Aida*, Radamés is condemned to death and sealed in a deep vault. Aida has hidden herself in the vault in order to die with her lover. The two perish in each other's arms.

around the rim of a phonograph record, with the summit the spindle. In fact, the route's vertical cross-section resembled a cardiogram, and the hike resembled walking around an octopus, having to surmount each leg.

Of course, one does things with a comrade that one would not think of doing alone. In 1987, after my friend Philippe Guilhemotonia and I had climbed Liberty Bell, instead of going directly home we stopped off at the Sauk River, where we walked along the shore in search of his wedding ring. He and his wife, Catherine, had started their honeymoon paddling down the Sauk. When rapids appeared, the alarmed bride capsized the canoe. Struggling to shore, Philippe lost his wedding ring from his toe, where he had put it because paddling chafed his finger. The dry summer exposed much river bottom, and we came upon some fishing lures, but found no ring.

Friends choosing to go into the mountains together for sustained experience, sometimes a single long expedition, sometimes a series of short ones, have their ties enhanced by the shared discomforts and challenges and also by what rarely touches those in other common endeavors: the beauties, magnetism, and magic of the mountains give the members a deep satisfaction, powerful welding, unforgotten pleasure and, for some, a sense of a Tamino entering the Temple of Sarastro.[21]

THE YOUNGEST ADVENTURERS

During the several years when I took my children into the mountains to hike and camp, I sought to enjoy their company while we did things that I like to do. But in further part missionary zeal moved me, a hope my sons and daughters, and sometimes nephews, would acquire the capacity and the taste for the outdoors. I thought it good for people: health, endurance of some discomfort, enrichment of soul, expanded and heightened aesthetic sense, perspective about the world by learning that there is more to it than streets and rooms, respect for nature, and a greater degree of harmony with the physical, "natural" world. Alas, I overdid, pressed them too hard, until

21. From Mozart's opera *The Magic Flute*, first performed in 1791. The protagonist, Tamino, must rescue the maiden Pamina from the temple of her mother's enemy, Sarastro.

to them the mountains meant fatigue, blisters, mosquito bites, rain, snow, and sometimes fear. I deluded myself to suppose these journeys constructive landmarks in the children's development. None became a wilderness lover, with the partial exception of Ben, who, in his brief twenty-four years, was a mountaineer. Their experience of the mountains added to their culture, however, and although they may grouch as they remember their discomforts, together we did have good times.

In 1956, Homer Harris (my friend since 1939), my son Fred, and I wandered through the Cascades, groping our way. One day we crossed some snowfields and went over Wenatchee Ridge, onto a shoulder of Bryant Peak and down to the Little Wenatchee River, inching our way over rocks and through brush, afflicted by bugs and heat. A couple of miles down the trail beside the river in the gathering dusk, we camped in the woods near snowbanks. Little Fred, not yet seven, toppled to the ground, where he slept for thirteen hours.

Along Icicle Creek in Leavenworth, where I journeyed with some of the children, little Dorothy spotted a footprint in the snow made by a member of the cat or dog family. Pointing at it apprehensively, she asked, "Is that a *paw*?" Often there was commotion and excitement among the children, who helped to gather firewood and vigorously frolicked. I hiked up Mount Si with Fred, age ten, and we were wet and cold under occasional snowfall. When we came upon a forlorn-looking mouse among the crevices near the top, he suggested, "Maybe it's an abominable snow mouse." Later I again found myself on Mount Si, this time with three children and under rain, snow, and hail. Ben, three and a half, sat on my shoulders. Going down he was unhappy and steadily cried, but he cheered up when dry and warm. When I was with my nephew/godson Jock Collins above Spray Park on Rainier, he amused me by glissading headfirst on his back. After a family journey through the central Cascades with my friend Homer, I noted, "I much prefer to drive myself to exhaustion than to have to stand still shuffling my feet in timid frustration as I so often do."

One spring day in 1961, three little girls and I hiked up to Trout Lake. The trail was not too steep, but slippery, and the snow crust would break every few steps. Dorothy, age five, cried the last mile and a half in the dusk, as she was tired, cold, and wet. It began to rain before we arrived at camp. I crouched on my knees over the faint fire, blowing on it, as the smoke enveloped my face and the rain ran down my neck. Dorothy kept warning me not to start a forest fire. It rained gently through the night. I spent the next morning getting the fire hot enough to cook and to dry the girls' pants and socks. We hiked back in the rain. Dorothy was magnificent in spirit and resolution. Jill was impressive and at ease; the conditions did not depress or discourage her. Cheerful the whole time, she had plenty of strength and was undismayed. I was a wreck.

In the summer of 1961 in the Olympics, I camped at the Dosewallips River trailhead with my daughters Ashley, Jill, and Dorothy and my nephew/godson Jock. I cooked supper, read to the children from *Captains Courageous*, and played the mouth organ for them. The next day we hiked up to Lake Constance, and the children were resolute good sports on that relentlessly steep trail. Dorothy, not yet six, plugged her way along the upper reaches with the tiny pack (her handkerchief its cargo) that she insisted on carrying, her thumb in her mouth and the other hand sometimes in mine, sometimes reaching for a crevice, a root, or a branch. Some of the children fished, without success, in the blue lake set among snow, firs, and crags. Jock and Jill slid down the snow slope. We spent two nights at the Lake Constance site, and on both evenings I read the children Jack London's story "To Build a Fire." After it, they felt cold. We were startled the first night by visits from goats, which had come near and watched us in the afternoon. From our sleeping bags, we threw pinecones at them to make them stop staring at us while standing at our feet. The fourth day we played and loafed around camp, and I read to the children before we hiked out. The descents on the rock were hard for Dorothy. We held hands, and I boosted, dragged, and braked her. She refused to be carried or to be relieved of her pack.

One evening, camped with the children above Icicle Creek, I placed Jill's boots—which had become soaked—before our fire to dry, while little Jill danced around with her arms above her head, singing, "I'm a little baby pea." Alas, I failed to pay proper attention. In the morning when she put her shoes on, the toe of one boot crumbled to ashes, so the poor girl had to hike with her toes poked out of her boot.

In 1968, Margaret, the youngest of six, and I hiked up to Talapus Lake with her kitten. When the time came to go home, the kitten could not be found. An intensive search followed; I didn't dare say, "Let's go." At long last, the kitten was found under a leaf. On return, we named the kitten Talapuss.

In the summer of 1972, my daughter Dorothy—then aged sixteen—and I set out to climb Sloan Peak in the North Cascades. The sun shone down on a cloudless, windless day. As we left the upper edge of the glacier, with a steep grade curving off out of sight, Dorothy became frightened. She had not yet learned self-arrest with her ice ax. On the last patch of snow, beside which I had taken off my crampons, she slipped, slid down the snowbank, then slid and rolled a few feet on the heather and rock, scraping her skin and upsetting her further. We walked a little way beyond along the steep heather slope at the foot of the summit castle, where she stayed while I went on to the summit. When a little way beyond and above her, I looked back and saw a 100-foot cliff just below where she had come to rest after her tumble and now sat calmly eating her lunch. I was mortified, realizing that if she had slid a few feet further, she would have been smashed far below. I should have put her on a rope for that stretch. We went down easily except for about an hour on the steep, damp, and brushy hillside where I lost the trail due to my poor sense of direction and poor place memory. Dorothy was a good sport the whole way.

In 1973, an eleven-year-old Margaret and I hiked in seven miles to Wallace Lake, where we had a picnic on a log that stuck out on the lake and picked and ate huckleberries, salmonberries, and blackberries. We took home a bag full, with which Margaret made two pies. Also in 1973, Margaret and I went out to climb Cadet Peak off the Mountain Loop Highway. We hiked up to Glacier Basin, then onto the ridge, with some rock scrambling on the way. It was a novel experience for her, and one she took as a good sport. After our picnic, we went on up the heather meadows. When she became weary, she stopped, while I went to the summit in a hurry. Coming down, I got off the rock castle and was on an easy grade in mixed snow, heather, and rock. Blue skies overhead, no wind, cool, silent, the fall colors at the lower altitudes, a fine day with my dear daughter—that's when I took the hardest bump in a long time. My feet went out and I slammed down, later finding welts and bruises between shoulder and knee. We went down and out, reaching the car as darkness fell.

Taking the children on mountain journeys would wear me down: I'd be bent under a load as the party packhorse, dragging a tired child with one hand and slapping flies with the other, carrying children across creeks on the stones, looking for lost children, puzzling over the route, answering incessant questions, and listening to incessant complaints. This effort on the trail was augmented by the tasks of camping: gathering firewood, building and tending fires, fetching water, washing up, unpacking, packing, protecting the food from animals at night, preparing a place to sleep and a shelter if it looked like rain, administering first aid for scratches and bites, smearing mosquito repellent on the younger ones, drying out their clothes when they fell in the creek, and so forth.

Of course, I made these excursions because I wanted to. They delighted me.

| 4 |

A HARSH CHALLENGE

*In the end we are better at the art of suffering,
and for high altitude this is everything.*

—VOYTEK KURTYKA, CLIMBER, ON WHY HE AND HIS FELLOW
POLES HAVE HAD SUCH AN IMPACT ON HIMALAYAN ALPINISM

FOR MOST MOUNTAINEERS, THE DIRECT and immediate pleasure
they get from mountaineering is joined by a sense of competition,
testing, and combat. Pleasure may lure us to the hills, but a harsh
challenge is what hooks us.

DANGER AND DISCOMFORT
Mountaineering's principal drawbacks are danger and discomfort.
Ironically, both also serve as major motives. A mountaineer is chal-
lenged to face the one and endure the other. They deter, yet draw.

As for danger, the second half of the twentieth century brought substantial increases in mountaineering safety, greatly increasing the number willing to climb. Yet to mountaineers, danger is also catnip. Joe Tasker, a British climber who made the first winter ascent of Eiger, wrote in *Savage Arena*, "Without the danger it is hardly likely that the superlative performance needed to overcome the difficulties would be stimulated."

Then there are the discomforts. A minor one is the tedium of camping: packing and unpacking, making and breaking camp. On the other hand, the perfunctory food preparation is less of a drag than it is at home (for those of us whose home food preparation tends toward the perfunctory).

Hard beds are another discomfort. A Scottish mountaineer told me of a cabin in his country where he and his climbing buddies would sleep on the "boonks"—all except for famed Scottish climber Hamish MacInnes, who disdained a "boonk." To "harden" himself, he slept on the floor.

A major mountaineering discomfort is exhaustion. On each of three expeditions to Denali, I was almost constantly tired, and many of the climbing days left me exhausted. I would welcome a storm for the chance it offered to rest. With perfect contentment, I would lie still all day, not even reading. When a party of Scots came clumping into camp at 14,500 feet, someone asked one of them, "How is it?" He replied, "Harrd wurrrk."

On other ventures, I often overdid. Seattle climber Dusan Jagersky and I climbed Jack Peak in California's Desolation Wilderness in the summer of 1975. As we approached the summit, clouds closed in and a light rain started to fall. We managed to get off the steep parts before the rock became overly slick. Twice we were lost in the fog and wandered about. We got home at 4:20 the next morning. To make this summit was satisfying, but not the way it was done.

Another discomfort is cold. Whether the cause is insufficient heat radiation, convection, conduction, or evaporation, it feels about the same. One takes measures to reduce this discomfort, but often it cannot be escaped. Four times in my life I have grown whiskers: once during the invasion of the Philippines, and three times during expeditions to Denali. In the Philippines, military discipline did not compel shaving, and in the Denali expeditions, not only was shaving inconvenient and not called for by social convention, but whiskers insulated the face a bit. There are other warming tricks as well. When he was writing about digging a snow cave in hard snow to escape the icy wind, the redoubtable Kurt Diemberger recalled, "An old bivouac rule says, the longer you prepare the bivouac, the shorter you need to spend in it."

I've never heard of mountaineers using the method to reduce the misery of cold that I once employed (not enjoyed) in 1940, while heading homeward on a westbound freight. Locked boxcars compelled me to resort to riding a flatcar. That night, in Minnesota, three other lads climbed aboard. The frigid wind swept us where we huddled on our bundles in the middle to escape being lurched off. In the darkness, never having seen each other's faces, we nonetheless arranged ourselves in a row, each leaning back against the chest of the one behind him, each with his arms around the one ahead. Thus passed the night. Reaching Fargo the next morning, we were all arrested. I used another method a couple of years earlier while passing through the Cascades, again on a flatcar. I was driven by the cold to open my suitcase and put on the clothes it contained, the last being my pajamas, and then to walk up and down the car swinging my arms.

Heat can also cause significant discomfort, although for me this has been much less of an occurrence than cold. Once, at 11,100 feet in Alaska, the tent thermometer registered 112 degrees. Such a phenomenon in the mountains is rare indeed, and brief; the mountaineer's experience is more likely to evoke that of the Klondike prospector thawed out in a furnace in Robert Service's ballad "The Cremation of Sam McGee."[22]

Much of the time discomfort is caused by bad weather, largely unforeseeable and so taken as a gamble. But often discomfort is caused by negligence. Forgetting to bring the stove makes one hungry, for instance, in which circumstance the coldness of the tent isn't even noticeable. When the error is yours, discomfort is compounded by embarrassment, which may long endure. In 1968, longtime friend Bagley Wright and I, with three of his young children

---

22. A 1907 poem in which the title character requests that his companion, the narrator, cremate his body if he doesn't survive the cold. After McGee freezes, the narrator attempts to cremate him but can't stand to watch. After returning, he is surprised to find McGee awake and smiling by the fire.

and one of mine, headed up toward the Enchantment Lakes. After a few yards I lost the trail, and we spent the rest of the afternoon trying to make our way upward without it. Impenetrable brush, downed timber, boulders, loose rock, briars, unscalable cliffs, steep and slippery hillside, mosquitoes, heat, and thirst combined. Two children despaired, vomited, and wanted to stop. At sunset the Wright family sat down and refused to take another step. (They had done so several times before, but this time they persisted in their resolve, or despair.) My son and I went in search of water, leaving them among the boulders, where they spent the night without campfire or dinner and with nothing to dampen their parched throats except Bagley's bottle of whiskey. I'm grateful that our friendship survived.

One of the most uncomfortable climbs I ever took was a long and strenuous three-day ascent (my third try) of Dome Peak in the Glacier Peak Wilderness with my friend Don Portman in the fall of 1977. A load of new snow at the summit created some avalanche danger in a couple of spots on the glacier and unstable footing on the rock. I should have had more sense than to undertake this before my broken ankle had healed (a year later, surgery corrected it). Every step hurt.

According to the common saying that it never rains but it pours, discomforts tend to come bunched. In the summer of 1995, when I was seventy-six, my friend Chris Maier and I enjoyed a set of discomforts plus failure when we undertook the Northeast Buttress of Goode, in the North Cascades. After the hike around, under a threatening sky, and a scramble up snow, scree, cliff band, slabs, and more scree to the foot of Storm King Glacier, we bivouacked on sloping rubble. The next morning, which took a long time to come after a night-long downpour, we scratched the climb and started down in the chill rain. For the last of our 900 feet of rappels, my injudicious choice of location put us in, through, and under a waterfall. Our seemingly endless journey continued as we staggered under our soaked packs, until at last we subsided in the brush by the road to Stehekin. When I arose in the morning, an affliction of dizziness made me fall flat.

In 1987, after Alex Bertulis and I had done the North Face of Shuksan (also in the North Cascades), already weary, we found our descent from the glacier to Price Lake to be an endless series of vegetable rappels, clambering over and under branches and logs, down and over slippery rock, all in the rain. At the creek, we found that the log and stick dam on which we had crossed the day before had washed away. The borders were brush-choked, so our search for a crossing meant we had to endure more of what we had been going through. After fifteen hours on the go, we spent the night beneath a boulder on a slope studded with big stones. In his spot, Alex lay on bigger stones, but in my spot, the overhang was so low that I could not turn over. The next morning we managed to cross the creek on a slender log, taking the packs across by ropes.

In 1989, I was climbing the West Ridge of Forbidden Peak with two visiting Lithuanian climbers when we were benighted on a ledge. We addressed our condition in different ways. Dainius Makauskas (who the following year died on Dhaulaghiri) calmly placed rocks, selected for their flatness, in a mosaic on the snow, lay down, and peacefully slept. Hunched on my pack, back against the cliff, I alternately dozed and shivered. The third member of our party kept warm by doing jumping jacks.

Mountaineering discomforts not only inflict their direct displeasures but also impair conversation. Voytek Kurtyka, the distinguished climber of 8,000-meter peaks, told me that on long expeditions the conversation of the first three weeks concerned women, the next three weeks food, and thereafter bowels and headaches.

FAILED ATTEMPTS

Everyone who has done more than minimal mountaineering has had a share of failed attempts. My own were many. Starting too late, getting lost, losing the way too often or for too long to enable making the summit; inability to find the way; rain, snow, mist; avalanche risk, rockfall, inability to accomplish a move up the rock; and so forth. Some routes on some peaks are apparent, regardless of their level of difficulty. Others are mysterious. After most of the failures I returned and made the summit, but some took many tries.

In 1973, I undertook to climb Mounts Buckner and Logan in the North Cascades with my son Ben and his friend Mark. We hiked in eight miles and camped in a meadow near Park Creek Pass. On the way up Mount

Buckner, when we started up the glacier we discovered that Mark had not brought crampons, so he and Ben each wore one of Ben's. At the glacier's upper edge we jumped across the moat onto the rock, climbed to a ledge where we left our crampons and ice axes, and went on up to the crest of the ridge, where we turned back—twelve hours on the go. The next morning we sought to climb Logan. We took a grossly mistaken route, which we avoided on our return. By the summit castle, the climbing conditions—the exposure, angle, loose rock, and thin holds—belied the guidebook's description of "an easy rock scramble." Without time to search for a better route, we beat a retreat. Two years later, I returned with Dusan Jagersky and we did Buckner expeditiously, then Booker Mountain as well. I returned again with two other guys. We approached from the north and did Logan with ease. As it turns out, the correct route helps a lot.

One may lose the way with or without a trail. One problem is no trail; another is a trail that does not go where you seek to go; still another is a multitude of trails that seem to offer equal probability of fulfilling your hope. On some humiliating occasions one may follow a route—trail or not—that twists here and there but returns to where you were before, as though you were treading a Mobius curve. On descent from California's Jack Peak in thick mist, my companions and I were chagrined to discover our own fresh tracks, going our way. Such a circuit may be a charming journey, if you are in no hurry.

In 1974, my son Ben, then seventeen, and I undertook to climb Bonanza in the North Cascades. We rode a truck up to Holden, hiked in to Holden Lake, and then climbed to the open slope between the timberline and the Mary Green Glacier. After searching for a place level enough to lie down, we dug and scraped the stones to make two spots, which looked like graves. After dinner we slept under a starry sky. The next morning we walked up the glacier on crisp snow, then continued up onto the ridge to the northwest, across a belt of snow above, over the ridge crest, and westward along the mountain's north face. With slow and careful pace, we traveled up a gully that combined steepness with loose rock and occasional rockfalls. Volleys and thunders of jagged cannonballs whizzed past, making us feel like pins in a bowling alley. On reaching the ridge where we entered the sunshine, we found that a cliff barred us. Realizing we had taken a wrong route, we retreated. I felt anxious creeping down the gully. A falling rock cut our rope most of the way through. My grab for a hold dislodged a loose rock that cracked my hard hat. Later the rocks went out from under my feet, and my attachment to the slope was kept only by a lunge for another hold, which held. We hiked down and out.

A few weeks later, Franz Gabl (a former Austrian Olympic skier) and I tried to climb Mount Pugh on the Mountain Loop Highway. After we left the trail through the woods and went upward on the snow, rain began to fall, then snow. Fog shut us in so we could not see our mountain and did not know where the summit was. We thought we were nearing the top only because we thought we were far from the bottom. We turned back because the snow slopes were getting steep and Franz had not brought an ice ax. (On our way down, he spoke about his experience as a machine gunner in the Wehrmacht for four years on the Russian front.) Later—when we returned to make the climb, without difficulty this time—we discovered that we had turned around far below the top.

The next month Franz and I tried to climb Colfax, one of the Black Buttes, on a shoulder of Mount Baker. As we neared the top of the ridge, about ten feet from us a snow plug that was about an eight-foot cube dropped with a roar into the crevasse it had concealed. Given pause by this, we turned back, frustrated at having come so near the summit.

On the way down the glacier after another defeat on Colfax, my nephew John Viste fell into a crevasse. He landed on a ledge and promptly climbed out. He asked me what I had been thinking as I anxiously hastened down to the edge before his head appeared. I told him, "I was wondering what I would tell your mother." On my third try of Colfax, again with Franz, we made it with uneventful ease.

So often did I fail to find the right way up a peak—Crater Lake's Garfield and the Three Queens in the Alpine Lakes Wilderness, among others—that after climbing Star Peak in the Cascades, I noted that I "was pleased with myself for accurate route finding (for once). Found the best possible route by map, compass, and looking at the land, so that I took the right route the first time rather than going by hit or miss with lots of misses." When one is in search of a geographical object, the compass often seems to be wrong. But it's wise to heed the saying "The compass does not lie."

FEAR

Nerve can overcome fear, reflecting moral self-control. One kind of nerve is tested when you make a choice. Another kind of nerve, less cerebral, more intestinal, is tested when you perform an action that poses a threat of immediate harm, e.g., making a move where you feel on the edge of slipping and the last protection is insecure and far below.

Most who undertake mountaineering find that fear of heights, natural in almost everyone, declines with experience. Also notable is that early in the process of learning to climb, slipping off one's holds a few times, after first informing one's partner who is belaying, can be constructive. Without experience in falling and being caught with no more drop than the rope stretch, a beginner may be too timid to make moves that may fail. With the reassurance from the gentle falls, the beginner will try harder moves and so discover the boundary between what will hold and what will slip.

Nerve is most needed where one has no choice between danger and safety, but where danger must be accepted and action taken. The prime example is to proceed downward when you don't know where or how. As the Polish climber Jerzy Kukuczka wrote, "The most frightening moment in the mountains is when one does not know which way to go." This proposition applies, of course, to descent (the context in which he wrote the sentence). Not knowing the way up may discourage or frustrate but not terrify. In contrast to many other causes of fear, the kind of fear caused by inability to find the way down is an experience but not a choice. One must get down. When Hornbein and Unsoeld made the first traverse of Everest, the route they had climbed could not be descended, so they had to find their way where they had never been. On his descent from Nanga Parbat, Reinhold Messner had a similarly harrowing experience. On the edge of death from avalanche, crevasse, or the cold, he had to find his way down the Diamir Face, where he had never been. In 2001, the Seattle Mountain Rescue group reported having come across "an apparent rappel anchor constructed from old socks" on the Mazama Glacier on Mount Adams. Such an image perfectly expresses the plight of trying to get down.

In the face of danger, decisions are made difficult or not based on the distance of the danger and the degree of choice. Often little choice is called for because such a large portion of the decision has been made far from danger—in distance and in time. When you reach the critical point—how will you get down this maze of crevasses and wet cliffs before you freeze?—often your only problem and only opportunity is exerting the will to act. If you cannot act at all, because no choice to do so exists, the only variations in conduct resemble those when facing fate: one's demeanor and self-control. On facing prompt and certain death, whether in a hospital or in a crevasse, about the only choice is degree of composure or breakdown.

Where choice is available, the best remedy for fear is justified confidence. Confidence can diminish fear, if not conquer it. And yet the principal limitation on performance seems to be not fear but overconfidence. What is needed, in British climbing pioneer Joe Brown's words in *The Hard Years*, is "the right amount of confidence"—enough to handle what you undertake, but not so much as to increase what you are willing to take. As climber and writer David Craig put it, it's about "enjoying the risk and respecting the danger." That is, measure what you can make your body do and conquer irrational fear.

Beyond the nerve that confidence brings, climbers need confidence to perform complex physical functions with skill. With confidence, you can still make your body do the things that fear would otherwise prevent. Confidence cannot give strength or stamina, but it can enable your body to perform the necessary moves.

Many climbers face their first fear on their first fairly difficult and exposed technical climb. They're safe because they're protected from above by the leader's rope; the fear is irrational, caused by the exposure. My first experiences of fear during climbing came on summit climbs of low technical difficulty, without exposure, unroped. I was with companions more skilled and more experienced than I. My fear was rational: slipping toward cliffs below. All that stood between us was a slope shaped like the outside of a ball.

For most people, confidence can be acquired by growing awareness of their capacity. For others, that may not be enough, because their lack of moral confidence impairs their confidence in their physical capacity. At the end of a long day in 1969, scrambling north of Snoqualmie Pass, up

Lundin and Snoqualmie Peaks and a couple of unnamed crags, I speculated on whether my fright at the steep spots meant that I had ceased wanting to kill myself or that I was simply cowardly in two ways: suicidal and scared of heights.

My achievements, moral and vocational, fell so far below my ambitions that they gave me scant satisfaction. They would evoke either indifference (if you can climb that peak, it can't amount to much) or disappointment. Whenever I entered the boxing ring, I felt: "Here I am, soft and sheltered, a privileged sissy, about to shuffle forward on this bright-lit canvas to fight that muscular athlete from the slums of Fightersville. I deserve to lose." I would lack both confidence and stamina.

In later years, at moments of doubt, a cartoon strip reminded me of this. In the strip, by Jules Feiffer, each caption lay below a drawing of the artist sitting on a summit. One caption spoke of how he climbed the mountain because he felt like a coward. Then, once he'd summited it, he thought it mustn't be much of a mountain. When the artist acknowledges his bravery to himself, he goes blind, but knows that if he admits he's a coward he'll see again. With only darkness above, the final caption reads, "All I ask is a couple of more hours on the top of the mountain."

| 5 |

THE PERSONALITY OF
A MOUNTAINEER

*Today's frontiers are not of promised lands, of uncrossed
passes and mysterious valleys beyond. . . . There are so many
ways, so much documentation, that only the mountaineer's
inner self remains uncharted.*

— PETE BOARDMAN, *THE SHINING MOUNTAIN*

MOUNTAINEERS TEND TO BE SELF-PROPELLED, self-reliant, thought-
ful individualists, with few team players. Most are competitive, but
not combative or contentious (except for some prima donnas on big
expeditions). Some are vain and selfish, others not at all.

Although many are introverts, it's doubtful they are introspec-
tive about their mountaineering. With most, it's a matter of finding
a climb that looks hard, then trying to do it. A substantial number of climbers are eccentric, although few to the degree of Ralph
Todhunter, a British climber and sometimes George Mallory partner, who wore white gloves while climbing. A psychologist's study

of thirty Polish mountaineers, mentioned in *Ascent* magazine, claimed that "two thirds exhibited a predominance of 'schizoidal personality. The whole group was characterized by weak sexual adjustment, weak social adaptation, uncooperativeness.' A Dream Team, if there ever was one." Though undoubtedly some eccentrics may be found among us, I believe the quoted conclusions are overdrawn.

Some scientific opinion holds that mountaineers are genetically different—though in just a small way—from all other people. Such evidence of determinism may console and reassure those mountaineers who fear being held responsible for their eccentricities. It should be said, too, that some mountaineers are unable to unwind; their engines cannot be idled. This makes the mountains an ideal destination for recreation because they call for almost perpetual exertion, and idleness tends to be uncomfortable.

Among hobbyists, nonprofessional mountaineers tend to be more consumed by their sport than all but a few fanatics. It can envelop all aspects of the mountaineer's life. Indeed, mountaineering probably generates more fantasies, brooding, daydreams, and frustration than any sport but golf.

RISK TAKERS

Some risks taken by mountaineers appear self-destructive. But people do not go into the mountains in order to step off a cliff, walk into a crevasse, or find a lump of ice on which to freeze as they sit. On Denali in 1992, a Korean climber, Dong Choon Seo, fell into a crevasse on the West Ridge. Severely injured, half-covered by debris, unable to move, possibly unsure of rescue, and, undoubtedly the most significant factor, suffering much pain, he sought to commit suicide by biting off his tongue. He was rescued and survived. I've never read or heard of a mountaineering death described as suicide. Some leading mountaineers have committed suicide, but outside the mountains. Italian adventurer Reinhold Messner wrote: "The Alpinist is not immune to suicide; but, as I see it, he never attempts it while climbing." He quoted the prominent nineteenth-century climber Eugen Guido

Lammer: "Anyone who is feeling weary of life should undertake a difficult climbing tour. . . . [O]nce he begins the dangerous ascent itself, he will be amazed to see how the urge to live seizes him. . . . "

Despite mountaineers' varied responses to risk, one perspective is shared by all: a desire to participate in the process and thereby to exercise some control over the risk. This makes the pursuit, in part, a game of skill with an element of chance.

The control element combines choice and personal capacity. Mountaineers keep a degree of control over risk by retaining the prerogative to choose their route or peak, and by exercising some personal capacity—such as strength, cleverness, coordination, endurance, balance, or cool judgment. A peak or cliff provides these elements, as can a tightrope walk, a solo transoceanic sail, or a nighttime swim across a lake. As Winston Churchill once remarked, "Play for more than you can afford to lose, and you will learn the game."

In some situations, a climber knows that if he slips, he will fall to his death. If he allows himself to slip, the fall will be his failure. Of course, there is a chance, and thus odds, that he will slip despite his efforts and care, even if he makes no mistake—from a failure of friction or a broken bit of rock or ice. He nonetheless feels the action and its results are largely in his control, and are not a bet on a chance.

PROFESSIONS

Only a statistically negligible number of mountaineers can earn a living from their sport, so many are employed doing something else. In comparison to the whole population, summit climbers are overrepresented among engineers, physicians and others in the health sciences, teachers, physicists, and mathematicians. Although they tend to be competitive, mountaineers are underrepresented among lawyers, salesmen, executives, and ex-athletes, all competitive groups.

Many mountaineers can be found in construction work, which involves well-paid and short-term commitments. Some are blessed by fortune to have a partner with an income who is patient and generous. Those who are not vagabonds or full-timers devote only part of their time to mountaineering, in the manner of those devoted to other sports.

A few addicts are out of the mountains so little of the time that they survive for periods in alternation between the back of their car and crashing with patient friends. Perhaps no one has carried this as far as Fred Beckey. Not until he approached his seventieth birthday did he buy a house, living in which was an unfamiliar experience. A friend called him late one evening. The phone rang for a long time before Beckey answered, and the friend expressed concern that the call had awakened him. "No," Beckey responded, "I was mowing my lawn."

"But it's dark," the friend pointed out. "How can you see where to cut?"

"Oh," said Beckey, "I just mow the parts that show under the streetlight."

No one involved with climbing earns the high income received by athletic stars in some other sports, and only a handful even earn a living from it. Of those who support themselves wholly by climbing, most earn their way as guides, and some as manufacturers' representatives or photojournalists. The stars earn money from books and articles, lecture tours with slides, and occasional parts in films. Superstars are paid to bless products. But again, from the many who aspire to fame and fortune, few are chosen.

PHYSIQUE

Rock climbing calls for hand and arm strength, but general "upper body strength," much discussed in the context of differences between the sexes, is not needed. By contrast, summit climbers need a strong back to tote a heavy load, pull a companion out of a crevasse, or push the car when it won't start on one's return to the trailhead.

Successful rock climbers have good technique, flexible bodies, and an acquired habit of prudent practices. Both summit climbers and rock climbers have good balance, rock climbers to a higher degree. Neither set is made dizzy by height, an immunity that can be acquired.

Summit climbers have strong legs, deep chests, and strength and stamina to carry loads in thin air. A good heart and lungs (with the stubborn determination common among summit climbers) can help greatly when going a long way upward on snow. A stranger I met on a ski lift once told me a story about his friend Gaston Rébuffat, a Chamonix guide and a leading twentieth-century mountaineer. One morning, as Rébuffat ate breakfast at an inn, a man approached him and asked to be guided up Mont Blanc. Rébuffat asked him if he'd climbed Mont Blanc before. "No." Other Alps? "None." What other mountains? "None." Rébuffat diplomatically suggested they go for a walk up the slope at the edge of town. The fellow did not stumble, so Rébuffat arranged to meet him early the next morning, surmising that, in an hour or two, their excursion would be finished in defeat. The man showed up, and they set forth. At their initial slow pace the man did not flag, so Rébuffat stepped it up, and the man continued without apparent difficulty. Curious, Rébuffat accelerated until reaching his top speed, an impressive rate. The man stayed with him, step for step, and did not puff. When the man began to whistle a tune, Rébuffat turned to him and asked, "Who in the world are you?" Answer: A Swede who, the previous winter, had won the Olympic gold medal for the 50k cross-country ski race. The two proceeded to the summit.

The time spread between fast and slow summit climbers exceeds that for rock climbers. Slow companions are not tolerated by fast, competitive summit climbers, who are unwilling to wait. In rock climbing, on the other hand, much time is spent waiting while belaying, so the added time of a slowpoke makes little difference. The main question is decided early: On the intended route, can you make the hardest moves?

Some mountaineers continue their sport at a high level despite suffering a partial disability. On Nanga Parbat in the Himalayas, Reinhold Messner lost a big toe and parts of several others (as well as losing his brother), yet went on with high achievement. Jim Wickwire continued Himalayan climbing after losing toes and suffering an impaired lung following a night in the high altitudes and extreme conditions of K2.

THE MIND OF THE MOUNTAINEER
Mountaineers' average intelligence (of the academic or abstract kind) tends to exceed that of athletes in other sports. And mountaineering tends to

require more thinking than do other sports. Some capacity for sustained concentration is needed for both safety and success. Few with bad judgment last for long. Rock climbers tend to have a lower level of formal education than summit climbers.

Some mountaineers who love the outdoors seek to learn the names of the plants and birds, perhaps feeling that closeness can be attained through words. The same goes for the few who study the scientific significance of the rocks they encounter as they go along. Primo Levi wrote of a hike through the Alps:

> *My passion for the mountains colluded with the passion I felt for chemistry, because there I found the elements in the Periodic Table embedded in the rocks, prisoners of the ice, and through them I tried to find the nature of the mountain, its structure, the why of the shape of a channel, the history of the architecture of a serac.*

Measured against good athletes in other sports, mountaineers, especially summit climbers, tend to have a more elevated level of culture. Proceeding upward with a single-minded ruthlessness, Jim Wickwire rarely pauses to drink in panoramas or sniff the edelweiss. Yet back in town, his tastes are cultivated; he derives pleasure from classical music, Keats's poetry, and Nabokov's mastery of English prose. And among his fellow mountaineers, he is far from alone in his tastes.

If one classifies thinking by reason, imagination, memory, and judgment, many mountaineers have high capacity in the first two. But it is their employment of the latter two that bears on their effectiveness as mountaineers. Two types of memory of past experience—a sort of mountaineering reference library—help. One is geographical memory, the ability to remember where you have been when you seek to retrace your steps. And another is memory of how situations—mostly forms of adversity—were handled, for better or for worse.

The other principal method of thought useful to mountaineers is judgment. More than in most other sports, mountaineering calls for good judgment, meaning capacity to measure the probable and comprehend the possible. (In this way, judgment is at odds with imagination.) Judgment is needed for rock climbing, in which one discerns and plans a route up a cliff, determining whether, where, and how. Judgment counts even more for peaks than for cliffs.

Good judgment is also applicable to forecasting weather, to estimate the time needed to reach waypoints and the summit and then descend to a safe place before weather, visibility, or fatigue imposes danger. One must be able to anticipate the unexpected. Summit climbing resembles ocean sailing in the importance of judgment. The quality of judgment affects whether you will suffer discomfort, get lost or get hurt, and obtain what you seek.

WRITERLY DREAMS

For mountaineers, writing books may be called an occupational habit. Mountaineers write more books per head than do participants in any other sport. Among those who produce books, most write their own, in contrast to many athletes from other sports whose names appear under book titles though they have not actually written a word. Measured against books written by or about athletes in other sports, mountaineers' books deserve a high grade. Measured by standards of good literature, however, their average quality is low. Some of the deficiencies reflect an insufficient literary education, by which I mean reading masters in the art and training to use the written word. Some show the amateur's lack of practice. Of all mountaineering books published, only a few display notable merit.

Why this widespread practice of writing books? For one, many mountaineers are readers. Most mountaineers could be called problem solvers, as they like to think things through, and many like to write down their jumbled thoughts in order to work through them. Sometimes these casual writings get carried on to print. Another contributing factor is that of temperament: those who write, like those who climb, stay much within their own minds. Like writing, mountaineering is a solitary task.

The mountaineer may write books to supplement his household's earnings, to publicize a lecture tour, or simply because others do so. Time spent immobilized in camp without other distractions of work or play also gives the mountaineer the opportunity to keep a daily journal, which serves as useful factual meat; events are fresh in memory, and entries on consecutive days show the logical connections of events.

A large proportion of the books by mountaineers are written for an audience of their fellows—an arrangement somewhat reminiscent of a country where all make their living by taking in each other's washing.[23] Jon Krakauer's *Into Thin Air* was an incredible exception, a popular and financial success far greater than any other American book on a mountaineering subject. As such, it provoked resentment and envy.

A few mountaineering books are well written by any standard. I have enjoyed British mountaineer Edward Whymper's nineteenth-century account *Scrambles amongst the Alps*, some of Bill Tilman's work, Belmore Browne's scattered writings quoted by Robert Bates in *Mountain Man*, Maurice Herzog's *Annapurna*, Gaston Rébuffat's *Starlight and Storm*, Tom Hornbein's *Everest: The West Ridge*, David Craig's *Native Stones*, and some work by John Menlove Edwards, Greg Child, and David Roberts, as well as Krakauer's *Into Thin Air*.[24] While these writings have merit, the same cannot be said for many others.

In their writings, some mountaineers assert a spiritual element. They wax on about how climbing offers them "a heightened sense of being . . . proof to us that we exist." Some ask "Why do we climb?" and go on about how the mountaineering experience reveals God's existence and intentions, the meaning of the universe, life's purpose, and other secrets unknown to those whom revelation has not blessed. Climbing peaks, they write, deciphers and illuminates life's meaning. Other mountaineer writers avoid the existential questions and attend more closely to their own state of mind. The hotshot climber Dean Potter told *Outside* how he felt on his free solos: "It brings me silence and peace, and I come closer to the pure me."[25]

Non-mountaineers with more powerful intellects have addressed these questions better than the authors of this incoherent mush. Why are we here,

23. This book is directed at *mes âmes amies*, some who are mountaineers and others not.

24. Although John Muir wrote superbly about the mountains and deeply appreciated their beauties, he did not write about mountaineers or mountaineering and, although he climbed Mount Shasta, Mount Rainier, and some other peaks, he was not himself more than an incidental mountaineer.

25. From the article "Climbing at the Speed of Soul" (December 2002).

Stim climbs 5.9 trad route Penny Lane at Smoke Bluff crags in Squamish, British Columbia. *(Photo by Cliff Leight)*

From left to right, siblings Patsy, Stim, and Harriet with mother Dorothy in the middle. *(Bullitt Family Collection)*

Stim, a college middleweight champion in the late 1930s, boxes with Eddie Cotton in the 1950s. *(Bullitt Family Collection)*

Pictured here in the Philippines in 1944, Stim served in the US Navy as a lieutenant during World War II. He was awarded a Purple Heart for a shrapnel wound received on Leyte. *(Bullitt Family Collection)*

Stim with three of his children, from left to right Ashley, Scott, and Jill, in his apartment at Grovenor House, 1954 *(Bullitt Family Collection)*

The Bullitt family celebrates
Stim's sixty-fifth birthday.
(Bullitt Family Collection)

(Bullitt Family Collection)

Bill Sumner, Stim Bullitt, and Jim
Wickwire at 14,000 feet on Denali after
turning back just short of the summit,
May 14, 1978 *(Photo by Jim Wickwire)*

Just above Windy Corner on the West Buttress of Denali *(Photo by Bill Sumner)*

Stim on the Kahiltna Glacier, Denali *(Photo by Bill Sumner)*

Stim and Shelby Scates on Kahiltna Glacier on the first day of a 1981 climb of Denali *(Photo by Bill Sumner)*

Stim descends from the summit of Denali after more than 24 hours of climbing. *(Photo by Bill Sumner)*

Fred Dunham, Tom Hornbein, Fred Stanley, Stim Bullitt, and Bill Sumner at the end of a day climbing in April 2007 at The Feathers, Vantage, Washington *(Photo by Tina Bullitt)*

Stim and his wife, Tina Bullitt, with climbing partner and friend Alex Bertulis in 2005 *(Photo by Tim Matsui)*

Stim and climbing partner Doug Walker prepare to climb at Exit 32 (Little Si), circa 2006-2008. *(Bullitt Family Collection)*

Stim and Tom Hornbein congratulate each other at the top of parallel routes in April 2007. The Feathers, Vantage, Washington. *(Photo by Bill Sumner)*

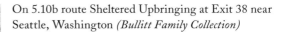
On 5.10b route Sheltered Upbringing at Exit 38 near Seattle, Washington *(Bullitt Family Collection)*

Stim, age 86, climbs Far Side Wall at Exit 38 near Seattle, Washington. *(Photo by Tim Matsui)*

On 5.10c route Booty Squirrel on Far Side Wall at Exit 38 near Seattle, Washington, in 2005 *(Bullitt Family Collection)*

Tina Bullitt commissioned this memorial sculpture, entitled *Illusion Dweller,* for Stim in 2012; visible only from the water, it stands on the shoreline of a natural area that Stim donated to Seattle Parks and Recreation. The plaque reads, "The loss of illusions, which goes with self-awareness, saves us from some folly while it takes away security and boldness," a quotation from Stim's book *To Be a Politician.* *(Photo by sculptor Gerard Tsutakawa)*

Stim, 83, with Tina Bullitt, returns from successfully climbing 5.10b route Illusion Dweller in Joshua Tree, 2002. *(Photo by Cliff Leight)*

why must we die, does any aspect of our personality continue after we die, or do we just become meat? These fundamental questions beset us all, but mountaineers' books, even the good ones, do not penetrate the mystery.

Mountaineers who write of their experiences often display faults common to many memoirists. Although it is said that no man is a hero to his valet, some men unquestionably are heroes to their autobiographers.

Occasionally mountaineering writers use their books to take revenge on colleagues and kin with vindictive knocks, from soft innuendo to virulent spite. A single such expression tends to impair the reader's confidence in the rest of the tale, just as a witness's single lie, caught on cross-examination, discredits in observers' minds a day of otherwise truthful testimony. The jilted climber might say something like "I deserved to be put on the first summit team. I stayed in top shape when others were getting coughs and headaches and making excuses; I carried more than my share of loads to stock the camps. But those two backstabbing sycophants, Sam and Pete, manipulated that weak leader to put them first, they made the summit, then snow fell nonstop for three weeks, and we all had to go home. If I see one on the street I'll cut him dead." An appealing contrast was an *American Alpine Journal* account of the first successful American K2 expedition, in which Lou Reichardt gave his companions liberal credit. (He did make the summit.)

Other writers' books contain a sensational display of personal matters properly kept private: "During the expedition, my car was repossessed because my wife couldn't make the payments, all having gone to that extortionate guide service." Still others disclose scandals about others: "That middle-aged socialite brought along excessive baggage and resembled an opera diva on tour with everything but a brace of poodles. She had a different thirty-year-old guide in her tent every night."

THE FELLOWSHIP OF THE ROPE

Climbers gather in boisterous carousing at Chamonix, Camp 4 (Yosemite), Talkeetna, Kathmandu, Leavenworth, Joshua Tree, El Potrero Chico, and other such places to celebrate the fellowship of the rope. They enjoy each other's company and share accounts of their experiences. Combining comradeship with competition, they boast: "And then I say to him, 'Stop whining, Reinhold, I got you up here and I'll get you down again. I can see you're not at ease at this level. Here, hand me your pack while we go up around this roof.'" "Well, last year I was making a new 5.14 at the Gorges du Verdon when my belayer got in a fight with a dog. You should have seen how I handled that one. But that's a long story." "Yeah, that reminds me of one time halfway up the Walker Spur, getting plastered with horizontal snow. My partner's hands were useless; he'd taken off his gloves to blow his nose or scratch or some fool thing, and they disappeared. Don't know how I ever got us out of that one." Others boast of epics that recall Shackleton on the Southern Ocean or Jason gaining the Golden Fleece. Or they boast of triumphs that rival Beowulf's when he confronted the monster Grendel, setting aside his weapons and armor before tearing off Grendel's arm (Beowulf wanted to make a proper sporting proposition; monsters don't have helmets or swords, only claws and fangs). Some of these reminiscences, often delivered in the presence of women, would remind me of carousing World War II flyers recalling, "There I was, flat on my back at 20,000 feet . . . "

In the CPO (chief and petty officers) mess on a small aircraft carrier during World War II, the chief torpedo men would appropriate some of the propellant fuel, grain alcohol (called "torpedo juice"), and mix it with canned fruit juice. This provided us with convivial occasions when we were off watch or at anchor. But these gatherings lacked the warmth of those among mountaineers. We chiefs shared some significant experience. We all wore the same clothes, ate the same food, slept in the same big bedroom (a compartment of forty bunks), did work similar in several ways, lived under the same rules, and underwent the same risks. There were some friendships, but on the whole the relationships had the same impersonality that they have at most workplaces. The big difference between these men and mountaineers at the same loud play is that mountaineers *select* each other, usually with some degree of friendship, and they are drawn together by the absorbing passion in which they delight.

It must be said that drugs are popular among young rock climbers. All is for pleasure, none for performance enhancement. I must confess, however, that I indulged in performance-enhancing drugs for non-mountaineering pursuits. During the years when I was competing as a ski racer, discouraged by my invariably poor performance, I obtained a prescription for a dose of speed from my doctor, who was bemused by my request. The next time we saw each other, he asked how it had worked. I told him that, as usual, I had arrived at the bottom—hill and finish rank—but with one difference: losing left me in good cheer.

Mountaineers' use of cigarettes has followed the changing practices of their nationalities. On a 1934 German expedition, for example, some members of the group smoked on Nanga Parbat—above 23,000 feet. In 1950, at almost 22,000 feet, the Frenchmen Maurice Herzog and Louis Lachenal relaxed with cigarettes. Now many Westerners abstain completely, while many Asians continue the practice once popular worldwide.

As to how much they talk, few mountaineers are garrulous, but they seem to reflect the range of the rest of humanity—from voluble to taciturn. In this aspect of personality, many are a pleasure, while a few are not. Edward Whymper commented in *The Ascent of the Matterhorn*: "[T]alkative men are hindrances: they are usually thirsty, and a thirsty man is a drag."

Some non-climbers envision the social side of mountaineering as a vast locker room, all crude banter, wet-towel snapping, and farting contests. Granted, boisterous jokes may be more common than elegant wit among the weary and preoccupied. Yet the relationship between mountaineers is actually complex. After all, they share struggles, hardships, triumphs, scenes of memorable beauty, and hilarious good times. They depend on each other not only for success, and sometimes recognition, but also for comfort, safety, and entertainment. This chemistry affects not only the pleasures, disappointments and satisfactions, but also the hazards. Even in the locker rooms of climbing gyms, one does not hear the coarse bragging and putdowns common to the locker rooms of other sports. Mountaineers do their bragging at occasions of dinner and drink.

INDIVIDUALISM

Mountaineers are spread across a wide range in their social outlook. Many are nonpolitical, indifferent to public policy, or (emotional) anarchists.

Those whom the wilderness delights tend to be conservationists. I have observed only a few who have located themselves on the liberal/conservative political spectrum.

Among mountaineers, the prevailing individualism and distaste for authority make leadership of a large climbing party difficult, which explains the frequent success of parties of four people or less. Such a group, if the members know each other and have equivalent ability, can operate as a partnership, without one person in command—something that would not be possible in a car, a plane, or a ship.

When Western climbers organize a big expedition, party members give their leader solemn and repeated assurances of fealty. Once on the mountain, however, they tend to indulge their individualistic impulses and habits. It is hard to understand why anyone would choose to lead such an expedition: no pay, dull work, absence of any strong levers of authority, and the task of herding a bunch of anarchist/libertarian/defiant prima donnas who will likely undermine the leader and eventually write a book attacking him (or her). On her return from an all-women's expedition to Annapurna, a friend and sometime climbing companion told me, with relish, that the Sherpas' name for her party's leader was Yeti, after the legendary wild and scary Abominable Snowman. The adventure writer Walt Unsworth expressed a similar notion when writing in *Everest: The Mountaineering History* about the famous 1971 Everest expedition involving thirty-three climbers and thirteen nationalities: "Wild accusations flew in every direction and when the hapless [Günter] Dyhrenfurth [the expedition leader], a sick man, returned to Base Camp, acclaimed Swiss mountaineer Yvette Vaucher pelted him with snowballs, yelling, *'Voici le salaud!'*" ("Here's the bastard!") An oft-told tale about an international expedition focuses on the group's plane ride from Europe to Kathmandu. A German member walked up the aisle and addressed a British member with an insufferable grin: "Ve bead you at your national game," referring to the World Cup soccer result, at which the Brit replied, "Oh, that's quite all right, old chap. After all, we've beaten you at yours—twice." What a way to start their endeavor!

Yet these ambitious men are often saved by their intelligent awareness that without some group direction and cohesion, all will fail. They also possess enough self-control to act on this awareness. Probably the leader's job is tougher with Americans, among whom the sense of individual rights (versus sense of duty or deference to authority) is often greater than it is among other nationalities.

Economic and social envy is rare among mountaineers. They do not look on differences in equipment as some do differences in automobiles. Widespread among mountaineers is a sense of honor, a somewhat old-fashioned attitude that is scorned by both those who hold a utilitarian moral outlook and those who regard this sense of honor as elitist and therefore bad.

TASTES AND PREFERENCES

Mountaineers' tastes in climbs are diverse: long expeditions to distant monsters, weekends to charming groves and glades, ice cliffs, overhanging granite, big parties, small ones, solos, pairs. Some go for a jolly gathering around a campfire, while others are content clipped to a sling, shivering on a sloping ledge. Rock climbers differ on the aesthetics of routes. Many prefer a consistent level of difficulty, which may require a zigzag meander, while others rate higher the purity of line, such as a straight arête or a raindrop's path as it trickles its way downward.

Muir showed his own taste when it came to his ascent of Rainier: "[O]ne feels far from home so high in the sky, so much so that one is inclined to guess that, apart from the acquisition of knowledge and the exhilaration of climbing, more pleasure is to be found at the foot of mountains than on their frozen tops."[26]

Others find tedium on trails through what may seem an endless tunnel of trees. They prefer athletic challenge up among distant vistas, rock and ice, heather, and the dome of sky, where, as Alice Munro wrote, "life is a flag unfurled."

Compared with competitors in other sports, mountaineers have tastes that tend toward the austere. Certainly some other sports call for training routines that are more arduous and dull. But mountaineering entails far

26. From *Steep Trails* (1918).

more days and nights, often weeks, of greater discomfort and tedium than anything on the playing fields and courts.

THE COSTS OF AN ADDICTION

Mountaineering diverts time from responsibilities to family and society. Careers are often impaired by neglect, and domestic breakups result from absences and anxieties inflicted on those near and dear. Alan Rouse (who later died on K2), high on Everest, was shivering on Christmas Day when he made a toast. He raised a mug of Scotch and, with characteristic refinement of expression, offered: "Here's to all the men in bed with our women." While early nineteenth-century whalers were away for a year or more, with similar risk and worse food, their absences were perhaps more forgivable because they were supporting their families and themselves.

As to civic responsibilities, mountaineers have done their duty to their country when it goes to war, but mountaineering tends to keep them from attending to the welfare and interests of their home communities. Those who devote most of their time to mountaineering contribute no more to society than do those with inherited, unearned income, who devote their lives to country club verandas, personal trainers, and charity balls. When Pericles dedicated the cemetery for the Athenian dead in the Peloponnesian War, he declared, "We do not consider one who takes no part in civic affairs as harmless, but as useless."[27]

There are exceptions, of course. Once, on a trail near the bottom of a mountain, I came upon a man bent beneath a giant sack so that he resembled Santa Claus. The sack was filled with bottles, pop cans, and other litter, which he had picked up and was taking out. He was a homely, lower-middle-class man. That a person who had comparatively modest pleasures available to him in life would still make this effort of civic generosity greatly struck my imagination. (This was before environmentalism had become politically correct.) I felt honored to live in a community and a society that

27. From "The Funeral Oration of Pericles" in *The History of the Peloponnesian War*, written c. 431 BCE by Greek historian Thucydides.

could produce such people. Part of my gratitude to him was due to my own love of the mountains. I don't know how I would survive without them.

Mountaineers who have responsibilities and yet take risks are doing wrong, as are mountaineers who devote more time to their engrossing pastime than may be properly allotted for a fulfilling hobby. Not only do they devote excessive time to an indulgence that gives pleasure to them but nothing of value to anyone else, but they take risks that nevermore will they furnish to others' economic, emotional, or intellectual value. After having been brought up and educated, they shirk their duty to their community. They inflict the heaviest burden, of course—anxiety and fear—on those who need, love, and miss them. Families may fear that they will die, experience anxiety during absences, and suffer periods of uncertainty about whether or not they are alive. Compounding these are the fear of losing the mountaineer's affection to some distraction on the stretches between home and the hills. Even at home, the near and dear have to endure the mountaineer's delayed reintegration into home life after return and his absorption as he prepares for the next venture.

Mountaineering addiction does not ruin the addicts' lives, except for sometimes cutting them short, but it tends to impair the lives of those who need them. Like the slave to crack, the mountaineering addict may live to regret his neglect of other responsibilities. No twelve-step program is available to break the habit.

In the winter of 1986, as described by climber and writer David Craig, a British "father and son were climbing in Glencoe. The son, aged fourteen, saw his father fall two hundred feet to his death. Then he had to perch for two hours on a ledge giving Mayday signals with his torch to attract rescuers." In 2000, an avalanche on Shishapangma in Tibet killed Alex Lowe, the leading American climber of his time, who left his wife and three young sons. (Roped to Lowe was his friend Conrad Anker, who survived the avalanche, married Lowe's widow, and adopted the three sons.) When Steve Risse, disregarding avalanche warnings, went up a British Columbia gully where an avalanche killed him (and two companions), he left a loving wife as well as grieving friends. Mrs. Dainius Makauskas lost to climbing accidents both her husband and her brother. In the two-week period back in England after soloing Everest, Alison Hargreaves was preoccupied with interviews and a sponsor, except for "one 'fantastic' day spent with her two children at the beach."[28] Then she set forth for K2, made the summit, and died in a storm on the way down.

Even if he does no other harm, the mountaineering addict inflicts anxiety. Joe Tasker wrote in *Savage Arena* that his partner Pete Boardman's "girlfriend had returned to Australia when she had overheard him by chance discussing with a friend the possibilities of climbing Changabang, before ever he had mentioned his plans to her."

Among well-known climbers, George Mallory, able but reckless, appeared to have considerable comfort with risk. Beautiful in body and face, he was athletic, intelligent, graceful, candid, enthusiastic, charming, mercurial, and vain. Unlike many athletes in other sports, he had friends and companions who became distinguished intellectuals: Lytton Strachey, Rupert Brooke, John Maynard Keynes, Robert Graves, Wilfred Blunt, Herbert Read, and more. Romantic, impractical, and naive, he lacked judgment. A child of his time and class, he bore social attitudes that if expressed today would label him a snob. Open-minded and sensitive, he had idealistic concerns for social justice.

His vigor and competitive drive made him an outstanding climber, but his early death exaggerated his importance. True, the dramatic manner of his death (he and his partner disappeared while close to the summit of Mount Everest, and his remains were not recovered for decades) gave it more symbolic significance in mountaineering history than if he had met his end in a hospital bed from an intersection collision, colon cancer, or a stroke. But like John and Robert Kennedy, Rupert Brooke, Antoine de Saint-Exupéry, General Louis Desaix, Nathan Hale, Joan of Arc, Icarus, Bruce Lee, and many obscure, dashing lads whose early deaths grieved their parents, Mallory's snuffed-out vitality makes his memory glow. We remember such young men longer and more vividly than those of equivalent achievement who lived on to display their frailties and become objects of sympathy, indifference, and scorn.

28. From an interview with journalist Alison Osius.

I myself have been affected by the costs of mountaineering. The day after a fall from Liberty Bell broke my ankle, I attended the memorial ceremony for friends Dusan Jagersky and Al Givler, killed two weeks before. We had been planning to attempt a new route together on Denali a few days later.

| 6 |

BREAKING ILLUSIONS

The top . . . was simply an end to the struggle upwards. . . .
No anthems played in my head. I only wanted to get down.

—Joe Tasker, *Savage Arena*

Several misperceptions exist regarding mountaineers, and I will endeavor to examine them one at a time. While mountaineers may dwell in illusion, there are also illusions *about* them that must be remedied.

THE VIEW FROM THE TOP

Non-climbers commonly suppose a climber's goal to be the view from the summit. Even for the sturdiest of legs and lungs and the most aesthetically sensitive of eyes, few views from summits are worth such hard work. Risk, discomfort, and effort are too high a price for a pleasing mountain view, many of which can be had with a ticket and a roof overhead. Although the view from a modest peak located in a range may be splendid, looking across at other peaks and down into lovely valleys, you can get that by going only halfway up. John Ruskin wrote, "All the best views of hills are at the bottom of them."[29] For a lofty summit or one set off by itself, like Denali, Rainier, Orizaba, Hood, and some of the Central Asian monsters, the view resembles that seen from an airliner window: drab, flat, and vague.

Non-climbers may suppose that jubilation is evoked the moment the summit is reached, that the climber takes a casual and relaxed glance around and tosses off some aphoristic comment on the feat. But most climbers feel no joy, even if the prospective descent is not arduous or difficult. Bill Tilman wrote in *The Ascent of Nanda Devi*, "It is seldom that conditions on top of a high peak allow the climber the time or the opportunity to savour the immediate fruits of victory. Too often, when having first carefully probed the snow to make sure he is not standing on a cornice, the climber straightens up preparatory to savouring the situation to the full, he is met by a perishing wind and the interesting view of a cloud at close quarters, and with a muttered imprecation turns in his tracks and begins the descent."

Sir Thomas Malory wrote in *Le Morte d'Arthur*: "King Arthur rode up to the creste of the cragge and than he comforted himself with the colde winde." At the Everest summit, the Swedish climber (who eventually moved to Seattle) Göran Kropp thought only of how he now must ride his bike back to Sweden. As quoted by Fergus Fleming, Austrian mountaineer Heinrich Harrer recalled his and his partners' feelings at having made the first ascent of the sought-after Eigerwand:

> *Joy, relief, tumultuous triumph? Not a bit of it. . . . The storm was raging so fiercely on the summit that we had to bend double. . . . This was no place in which to turn handsprings or shriek with joy and happiness. We just shook hands without a word. Then we started down at once.*[30]

29. From a personal letter collected in *The Works of John Ruskin*, Volume 37 (1909).
30. From *Killing Dragons: The Conquest of the Alps* (2000).

My own diary entry on reaching the Denali summit after my third try read:

7/18/81, 2:45 AM. The thermometer read −34°. I felt no jubilation, no euphoria, no delight, no excitement, not even solid satisfaction—all the good feelings were postponed. The sun was just below the horizon, sending up a long red sunset/sunrise band, and above the other horizon a full moon hung. The sky was clear enough to let us see far, but we did not look much. After a few minutes, during which Bill rubbed Shelby's chilled big toe against Bill's bare chest to warm it, we headed down, eager to escape the risk of a weather change. . . . We were happy when we got off the face below Denali Pass; a portion was wind-slabbed, and the rest was deep and moderately soft. As we neared camp, my weariness became so great that I stopped to sit down every few steps. The other two arrived about nine in the morning and I ten or fifteen minutes later.

MOUNTAIN MASOCHISTS

Some non-climbers are convinced that climbers must be masochists. It is true that some climbers do not mind pain or discomfort as much as non-climbers, and many regard discomfort as a challenge. Nonetheless, I know none who take pleasure from pain or who even are indifferent to it, and only a statistically insignificant remnant who welcome discomfort.

Another illusion is that some experiences are dreadful, when in fact they are not. For example, when ascending the North Peak of Mount Index in the Cascades with Alex Bertulis, and when descending Exfoliation Dome in the Darrington area with my friend Philippe Guilhemotonia, we spent a night anchored to a cliff to keep from sliding off. The night involved a cycle of sleeping while gradually sliding, then being awakened by the pull of the rope, and hitching upward to resume sleep. Sure, this warn't no feather bed, but it was not memorably horrid. We were neither cold, wet, or scared, nor afflicted by exhaustion, hunger, or thirst. Nothing hurt. It may sound terrible but it was not, and the experience did not make us masochists by any stretch.

"A GOOD DEATH"

Some say of a mountaineering death that the victim was "doing what he loved," as though such a death is somehow less of a dirty trick. Nonsense! For him whose life has been snuffed out, did the mountaineering that gave him such delight need to include being killed? Was he fulfilled by shivering lost and huddled on a wet log? By stumbling numb, by spinning in accelerating somersaults, by gasping for breath as his lungs gurgled, by hurtling toward rocks? Or being wedged in an icy cleft, deep in a dark, chill cavern? If a sudden fire barbecues a man, are his friends made to think the loss less grim by recalling that he was taken in a nightclub, living it up?

Recalling a moment high on Annapurna, his hands and feet frozen, French climber Maurice Herzog wrote in *Annapurna*: "I knew the end was near, but it was the end that all mountaineers wish for—an end in keeping with their ruling passion." I doubt that this wish represents either that of many mountaineers or even of Herzog. Rather, I think his deep feeling may have carried him away in a burst of grandiloquence.

In addition to the "doing what he loved" illusion, some hold to the notion that a mountaineer is blessed by some philosophic tranquility on the occasion of his death outdoors. I have had some near misses of death by accident, most of which injured me—auto collisions, enemy fire, rockfall, avalanches, and a number of climbing falls. None gave me the described sensations. All were sudden and brief. There was no moment for tranquil clarity. Each experience was "Uh-oh, bang!" And most mountaineering deaths, other than those of dwindling vitality, are sudden.

COURAGE

A few mountaineers and many who are not credit climbers with courage. They believe that doing something dangerous—whatever the circumstances—demonstrates courage rather than folly. This proposition is false. Whatever motives induce one to climb—single or multiple, conscious or unconscious, healthy or sick—they have one thing in common: they are for one's self. Like all sports, mountaineering is pursued to gratify those who take part.

Mountaineering risks can merit the term "courageous" only when the motive for taking them is *unselfish*—that is, when protecting or saving another involves a risk that person would not otherwise take. Rescues are acts of generosity or duty. Dangerous rescues are courageous and often inspired by loyalty. On big mountains and small, disasters are faithfully reported, while courageous rescues commonly go unnoticed after one and all are brought home safe.

Loyalty develops from a sense among mountaineers of belonging to a brotherhood (not sex-specific) bound by mutual interests. You rescue the fellow traveler in desperate straits, whether a stranger or your pal, sympathizing with his plight and hoping you would be treated likewise if you found yourself in his shoes.

As we neared the summit of Denali on my first try, I became exhausted, began to stagger, and often fell. My companions, Jim Wickwire and Bill Sumner, turned around, and we retreated together. If they had gone on, they would have made the summit (something Wickwire already had done and would do again, and Sumner would do twice later) but would have left a companion and friend to freeze (it was cold). These two men's characters and loyalty I admire. By reason of their background, experience, and membership in the climbers' brotherhood, however, their action on this occasion evoked my approval but not applause. This was duty, not courage.

Fundraisers for an expedition to some Himalayan monster often present the trip's purpose as support for an exalted cause. The climbing party, a crowd of hard-driving young sportsmen, is portrayed as warriors pursuing some noble grail. According to journalist Fergus Fleming, "Mussolini struck a *Pro Valore* medal for those who completed a new Grade 6 *direttissima* ascent. Hitler, more reserved, offered a handshake." In fact, these mountaineers' purposes are respectable, but they seek personal, selfish ends. A contribution to such an endeavor no more qualifies for an IRS deduction than does a gift of tennis balls to a tennis player friend.

Suppose the rules of golf were amended to permit games to be played only during thunderstorms. Should we admire those whose addiction put them on the links, their life insurance policies written only by Lloyd's? Should we credit them with courage comparable to those on tankers during war?

If "courage" includes strenuous and risky efforts to surmount geo-graphic features for fun, the word becomes blurred. Such an expanded definition debases the language, romanticizes recklessness, denigrates the term for a noble quality, and may delude some climbers into taking risks they would not take if they realized that not "courage" but "daring," "nerve," "determination," or "fortitude" was a better-fitting label for what they displayed.

Rather, "courage" should be defined as an act that exposes one to the risk of paying a price for some person or cause beyond oneself. Then the quality of that act should be measured by three things: the size of the price, the odds it will be paid, and the actor's degree of choice. The price may be anything undesirable to lose, such as life, liberty, love, fortune, honor, or exemption from pain. For instance, one may risk impoverishment by guaranteeing a friend's debt. Or one may risk loss of job, reputation, and friends by asserting a proposition others hate.

A top score in courage was earned during World War II by Sadao Munemori of the 442nd Combat Team, posthumously awarded the Medal of Honor. All three "courage" measurements applied: the highest price, cer-tainty of payment, and a clear choice. In a trench in northern Italy, a young man with a long life ahead of him, he threw himself on a German grenade. He had a chance of survival by diving in the opposite direction, but chose to save comrades and was blown to bits.

The price of death may be adjusted by life expectancy. Accepting death does not mean accepting mortality—which applies to all. It means *giving up* one's life expectancy. Those who are older and accept death pay a far smaller price than does a young man such as Sadao Munemori, because they had such a short life expectancy. The odds that the price will be paid also affect the score. Certainty gets the highest score, then high risk, then remote risk. High-risk odds cover most winners of the Victoria Cross and the Congressional Medal.

And, of course, one must be faced not with necessity but with choice. The wider the choice, the higher the score. During World War II, an Australian pilot of a two-engine plane made some boldly effective, low-level bombing missions over Japanese positions in New Guinea. He was identified, and the radio broadcasts declared that if caught he would be executed. He chose to continue daily missions and was shot down, captured, and beheaded. The same type of choice was made by James Meredith, an African American activist who started the March Against Fear, a walk from Memphis to Jackson in 1966 to protest racism. Meredith was shot shortly after starting the march, though he recovered in time to finish it.[31]

In an Australian trench at Gallipoli in World War I, Victorian Cross recipient Bill Dunstan fielded incoming hand grenades and threw them back at the Turks. Dunstan, whom I knew as an unquestionably brave and admirable man, exercised supreme nerve, but his alternative had been to let the grenades go off at his feet. (I commented to him that I did not envy his sons, serving in the European theater, because they must feel pressed to keep up with Pop. He responded with what probably was a half-truth, that to his boys he was an old codger in carpet slippers.)

The moral quality of our conduct can be judged in different ways, and often is. I took a public stand against the Vietnam War, which was praised for courage by many and attacked as cowardice by many others. My support of the proposed King County Charter in my 1952 race for Congress was praised for courage by attorney-activist Jim Ellis and went unnoticed by everyone else.[32] Neither act took moral effort by me; other actions (my boxing matches, running for Congress against former senator Hugh Mitchell) did, but were not praised for that. My volunteering for the Leyte beach party during World War II is the sort of thing that might have been praised, but no one did so. To volunteer took no moral effort on my part, and I likewise did not admire the men in my unit who also had volunteered.

In every one of my amateur (plus one professional) fights, I could not make myself enter the ring without exerting moral effort, but this was no issue of courage; it owed to lack of confidence and nerve. Once, in the Bronx Coliseum, in the Diamond Belt tournament, an amateur fighter (who had been described in the sports page report as "a powerful Negro from Brooklyn") licked me. The newspaper said of me: "Blood ran from his nose

31. Stimson gave scholarship grants to a number of minority students, including Meredith, who attended Columbia Law School.

32. The charter proposed "home rule" for the county, eliminating the three-member board of county commissioners (which had ruled King County since its creation in 1852) and replacing it with a seven-member county council and an appointed county administrator.

as he went to his corner at the end of the round. He fought with courage all the way through the third, yet . . . "

Now, this was not courage at all. It had something to do with playing a sport. If you find yourself on an oval track, you run; if you are in the ring, you fight. But it had nothing to do with taking a risk for another, or even taking a risk at all. The seventeenth-century French noble François de La Rochefoucauld once wrote in *Maxims and Reflections Upon Man*, "The love of glory, the fear of disgrace, incentive to succeed, the desire to live in comfort, and the instinct to humiliate others are often the cause of that courage so renowned among men." Granted, La Rochefoucauld tended to find self-interest behind all human actions. His cynical reputation might diminish the force of this maxim, but his words nonetheless underscore the uselessness of subjective measurements.

HEROES AT PLAY

Are mountaineers heroes? British climber Pete Boardman responded to this question by expanding it rather than answering it in *The Shining Mountain*: "What are mountaineers? Professional heroes of the West? Escapist parasites who play at adventures? Obsessive dropouts who do something different? Malcontents and egomaniacs who have not the discipline to conform?"

In contrast to courage, in which an act is admired, a hero is an image of personality—through memory, record, or legend—that inspires an observer to admire and, sometimes, emulate. To be a hero, all you need is a set of hero worshippers whose values idealize what you have to offer.

I have admired several people as mountaineers and as men, and I have been devoted to some mountaineers as their friend. None has been a hero in my eyes—in part because I have known them as humans, not superhumans. Likewise, no lawyer has been my hero (except for some judges and the movie part of Thomas More in *A Man for All Seasons*). A number of men have been heroes in my mind, inspiring in me a strong idealistic pull to emulate them, but none of my heroes has been a man I knew well. My pantheon has changed over the years, reflecting experience and thought.

Our ranking of those we consider heroes rises or falls throughout our lives as our lives modify us.

Another reason I never considered mountaineers heroes is that I found mountaineering not as tough as either boxing or war, though far more fun. I never headed for the mountains feeling like the "well-known Frenchman" quoted by the nineteenth-century writer Madame de Staël in her memoirs: "I tremble at the dangers to which my courage is about to expose me." I never, like young Henry V, addressed my comrades as we climbed out of the car at the trailhead:

> *Once more unto the breach, dear friends, once more;*
> *Or close the wall up with our party's dead.*

Those called "sports heroes" are named as such almost wholly from their achievement in sports, not from display of character (although I don't usually label as heroes high-achieving sports stars with bad character). I used to scorn men who had been athletic heroes when young but who did not grow up, remaining fixed back in "that championship season." I knew, for instance, a Seattle businessman who was a wholly decent fellow, but pathetic in his dreaming of the days when he was an all-American.

Now I wonder if I have been engaged in a kind of converse process, equally to be disparaged. Having so regretted failure as an athlete (football and boxing) when young, I continued to try for athletic success in old age, making efforts, consuming time, and seeking mountaineering scores, when my time would have been better spent using mind instead of body.

A hero differs from a role model. The hero's distinctive feature is to be larger than life, an exalted star. Heroes are socially useful because they inspire conduct of which we approve. Recently, however, it seems there has been a decline in recognizing true heroes, a phenomenon I find both puzzling and deplorable. Perhaps this decline comes from recognition of universal human frailty, or historical debunking. Or perhaps it stems from a cynical belief that idealism is for suckers.

| 7 |

RISK AND RECKLESSNESS

I need . . . abysses beside me to make me afraid.

—JEAN-JACQUES ROUSSEAU, *CONFESSIONS*

When one has no arms to help and no head to guide him except his own, he must needs take note even of small things, for he cannot afford to throw away a chance.

—EDWARD WHYMPER, *THE ASCENT OF THE MATTERHORN*

THE MOTIVATION TO TAKE MOUNTAINEERING risks comes from the satisfaction of self-reliance, the reassuring pleasure derived from success, and the sense of beating the game. In the long term, the process exhilarates and gives a sense of vivid living. In the short term, it's a "rush."

Risks that effort and skill cannot prevent are called "objective risks." Some examples are avalanche, altitude sickness, cold, and storms. The damage from objective risks, if taken, can be minimized by prudence and good judgment but wholly escaped only by luck. The other kind of risk that climbers can largely avoid is "human error."

For summit climbs, objective risks preponderate. For rock climbing, human error is the more common: recklessness, stupidity, ignorance, mistaken judgment, and, most commonly, negligence (in the sense of carelessness or inattentiveness, not neglect of duty).

The climber must ask a series of questions: How far can we go before dark? When will a storm descend on us? How will the temperature change? Will it get colder (feet may slip on rock, fingers may become too numb to hold tight)? Warmer (an avalanche, exhaustingly soft snow in which to flounder, a serac tumbling down on us)? Some err when they exceed the margin of strength, skill, or endurance under conditions that demand it for survival. An undramatic but real judgment error is to climb until no energy remains for the toil of making camp in severe weather.

In the matter of mountaineering judgment, sailing a boat offers a useful comparison. In 1992, attempting to follow Columbus's route (500 years later), I sailed a thirty-six-foot sloop out of the Mediterranean through the Strait of Gibraltar. In late afternoon, my companions and I were on the north (Spanish) side of the channel, with a stiff north wind. We planned to continue westward maybe thirty miles before veering southward on our way to the Canary Islands. We watched a steady parade of tankers and freighters move down the center of the channel. Reluctant to cross that fearful highway in the dark, I undertook to cross it forthwith and then to hug the African shore.

My big mistake was failing to consider that the wind might rise, which it did. Instead of safely kicking along the Spanish coast until the next morning, I had gotten us in a struggle to escape being driven ashore and wrecked on the African coast. The relevant chart showed a wavy line designated "Africa," with a dot designated "Tangier," the nearest port. The scariest moment came on looking out to starboard, as we whizzed along in the stormy darkness, to see us passing a big, unlit buoy. If we had hit it, we would have sunk like the proverbial stone. By the town lights, we zipped through the Tangier harbor entrance. It felt like turning into a strange garage at thirty miles per hour.

Although not a common cause, bad judgment is quite able to bring about a rock-climbing accident. My own judgment has never been good, although, with luck, I have avoided enough wild imprudence to have escaped disaster. My horrid judgment is rare enough that it does not contradict the general proposition that rock-climbing accidents are primarily due to attention deficit.

Risks that may be subject to severe consequences are real, though rare. One is a lapse of "situational awareness," a failure to look around and appraise the situation. When the climber finishes a taxing stretch and reaches a summit, a ledge, or an easy slope where no hands are needed to hold one's place, he pauses to unwind a bit, stretch, scratch, yawn, and coil the rope. But one heedless step on gravel, slimy moss, wet leaves, or a patch of ice, and he is done in. Lionel Terray, one of the world's ablest climbers, had climbed a cliff with his partner and reached the grassy slope above when one slipped, and down they went.

In 1977, after completing the first ascent of an unnamed peak in the Southeast Alaskan Coast Range by a hard route, Dusan Jagersky and Al Givler were descending by the comparatively easier steep snow slopes on the other side. Their companions, Jim Wickwire and Steve Marts, used the prudent and cautious, though awkward, method of facing in toward the slope and kicking steps with the toes, enabling each to use both hands to plant his ice ax. Jagersky and Givler, casual, faced outward, kicking steps with the heel. Wickwire and Marts heard a clink from above and saw their friends, roped together, tumbling past them, unable to arrest themselves as they gained speed. As they shot past rocks at a cliff edge they set off a shower of sparks, presumably from their crampons, vivid in the dusk. Their shattered remains dropped several thousand feet and were scattered on the avalanche cone. Each left behind a bright future and a loving wife. The style of descent was incautious, and the careless element was the stumble (by whom is unknown) that started the fall.

AVALANCHE

An avalanche is a major risk on most high peaks. It's a risk on *all* peaks where an open slope on an intermediate grade sustains a heavy snowfall and abrupt temperature change.

Although a sunny afternoon increases probability, possibility remains at all times. The roars of material coming down on Rainier and Denali and below Johannesburg Mountain (in the North Cascades) and Mount Shuksan (near Bellingham) have awakened me intermittently through the night. And sometimes they do not roar. Silent flows of new soft, fluffy snow have smothered many in their tents, some of them awake.

Avalanches have killed some of the world's best mountaineers, such as Anatoli Boukreev, Nick Estcourt, Dougal Haston, Alex Lowe, and Willi Unsoeld. Because their skill was high and their ambition compelling, they repeatedly exposed themselves to high risks. None was known for recklessness, however (if they were, they likely wouldn't have acquired their extensive experience). Everyone lapses into mistaken judgment at times, but at least some of these men's fatal accidents may be attributable to unavoidable chance.

On a warm day in 1981, my partners, Shelby Scates and Bill Sumner, and I descended the West Buttress of Denali. For a while, we sat on the crest at 16,000 feet, where we waited for the fallen snow—six feet of new— to stabilize. As we proceeded downward in the cool of the evening, we saw that an avalanche had swept the face. Tramping through the debris, we came upon a pair of ski goggles, then someone's eyeglasses, then a trail of blood spots, as though we were following a wounded animal, all the way to the camp area at the foot. We learned that three men from Barcelona had turned back at the crest when one had fallen sick. They had started to glissade, setting off the avalanche that all survived, one of them with a punctured groin and his face cut up.

Certain avalanche situations pose a low-risk sporting proposition. In 1967, during a light rain, I was on descent from the summit of Granite Mountain (one of the western Cascade foothills). While alternately walking, running, and glissading down a snow-filled gully, I started a small avalanche that got up enough speed to knock my legs from under me and put me in sliding snow to my waist. I squirmed over to the bordering rocks and watched the snow go past.

In early spring of 1980, Jim Wickwire and I camped at 9,700 feet at the foot of the Wilson Wall on Rainier. We were standing by our tent on an easy grade when, well above us, a slab split off the Kautz Ice Cliff, and broken blocks, ranging in size from a Volkswagen to a refrigerator, tumbled toward us as we crouched, hands on knees, like infielders at the moment of the pitch. But we missed the challenge of a jump to right or left, as all blocks passed us or slowed to a stop above us. A couple of months later, as we descended Denali's West Ridge, a soft-snow avalanche caught the two of us, but Wickwire held us fast as the snow flowed around our necks. When movement stopped, we were left with our shoulders at the surface. We struggled free, shook ourselves like wet dogs, and proceeded on down.

A few years later, as a group of us trudged our way up the Emmons Glacier on Rainier, a roar above froze us with fear that a slice of the peak was collapsing on us. A moment later, the ridge above was skimmed by two fighter jets.

HIGH-RISK SCENARIOS

In the mountains, glissading accidents, though infrequent, tend to be caused by ignorance of two things: braking technique and what lies below. Without knowing how to apply the brake, one may lose control, tumble and slide into rocks, or fall over a drop. To glissade is reckless unless one knows what lies out of sight below. One may encounter conditions that cannot be escaped by braking. One such condition (perhaps invisible from the point of decision to take off) is a slope that steepens so that a self-arrest will not stop the slider, and where below the steep place the snow does not offer a benevolent concave curve on which to slow to a stop, but rather a drop-off with something hard at the bottom. Another condition is a benign snow slope succeeded by slick ice, on which the would-be glissader accelerates like hockey star Howie Morenz going down the rink.

Crampons and glissades do not mix well. Snow hard enough to call for crampons for foot travel tends to compel intense braking for a glissade. Also, the risk is great that one of the heel spikes will catch, throwing the glissader into a somersault that starts a long tumble. That happened to a man descending from Mount Shasta in 2001. His ice ax "entered his thigh just below his pelvis and exited near his knee." The thought makes one's toes curl.

On a glacier, anyone risks falling into a crevasse. Prudent mountaineers conduct glacier travel while connected to one or more partners by a long rope. Renato Casarotto, the outstanding Italian climber, died of his injuries after falling into a crevasse during a solo attempt on K2 in 1986. Louis Lachenal of France was killed when he skied into a crevasse. What errors led these superb and experienced mountaineers to their deaths? Since recklessness may be defined as choosing danger without prospect of great reward, Casarotto could argue plausibly that, for a man whose life was dedicated to climbing achievement and whose experience enabled him to judge better than most where to go on a glacier, he was not reckless because the prospective reward of having soloed K2 was worth the risk. (More on this calculation in a moment.) On the other hand, Lachenal, out for a pleasant day in Alpine sunshine, and knowing well the risk of dropping into a crevasse, seems to have acted with clear recklessness. Some reports have suggested that his state of mind toward his life had turned to indifference—and thus recklessness. Famed American climber Terrance "Mugs" Stump, who was guiding on Denali, appeared to have lapsed into a moment of negligence when he failed to require his client next on the rope to take in slack and place a firm belay before Mugs explored the crevasse lip that collapsed beneath him, then upon him.

Big glaciers have few sure safe spots. The rope should never be slack. When I allowed slack on a Canadian glacier, Fred Beckey, a prudent mountaineer, corrected me with a sharp bark. Nor should the roped connection be set aside, except where the snow underfoot has been tested for a cavern beneath.

Like glissades, rappels appeal to many. Both speed one's descent. Rappels are more useful, glissades more fun. While glissading accidents owe more to ignorance, and most victims are novices, rappelling accidents commonly are caused by negligence.

Rappelling calls for a set of functions that are similar but essential: Select a firm anchor. Test it. Attach the doubled rope dependably to the anchor. Attach the rope to one's belay device and the device to one's seat harness, which is to be firmly fastened to oneself. Remain in control of one's speed on the way down. Remember not to slide off the rope ends if one reaches them while still high on the cliff. Many top mountaineers, such as Tom Patey, have been killed by careless error in one of these functions. Such errors commonly begin with a blunder and end with a thud.

Being harmed by falling rock or ice tends to be a matter of bad luck, to which judgment error sometimes contributes. Some is kicked loose and much comes "spontaneously," meaning from the weakening of what had attached the chunk to a larger piece of the Earth. In 1974, a family friend, Ian Black, who was about fourteen, was killed by a falling chunk of ice while hiking in Utah. In 1963, American climber Jake Breitenbach was crushed by collapsing ice blocks in the Khumbu Icefall. On the south face of Annapurna, the bold British climber Alex MacIntyre was killed by a falling stone. My friend and client Joan Webber, a Milton specialist in the University of Washington English Department and an experienced mountaineer, suffered an accident attributable almost solely to bad luck. On Papoose, a small peak on the side of Mount Rainier, during a scramble, not a technical climb, her group was climbing unroped. One of her companions above kicked loose a rock that fell on her head, knocking her off her feet, so she tumbled a little way. This killed her. Exposing herself to the chance that one of her companions would have made this careless error was the only risk she took.

By good fortune, I've never pulled out a rock big enough to scare or harm, except for the summer of 1986, on descent from Mount Sir Donald in the Canadian Rockies, after we had done the Northwest Arête. I dislodged a stone that rolled over my left foot, breaking a bone. On descent from Little Tahoma (a satellite peak of Mount Rainier), a stone the size of a cantaloupe dropped from above and hit me in the back; the protection of my pack left me alarmed but unharmed.

In the summer of 1980, during a retreat in an all-day rain from one of several failed attempts on Big Four Peak (off the Mountain Loop Highway), while we scrambled downward through brush, my companion dislodged a boulder, which rolled downward and over me. I drove to Swedish Medical Center back in Seattle and parked near the emergency room entrance late at night. I lurched out of the car, stumbled, and sprawled on the sidewalk. Then, seeing a couple of policemen approach, aware of my torn and shabby clothes and dirty and unshaven face, I heaved myself to my feet with effort, hoping they would not take me with them. They let me go in. Damage: broken left leg, sprained ankle, and some lesser items. I got checked out with a cast and crutches.

A high-risk area in which one does not want to spend any time is an icefall. This term refers not to falling ice but to wreckage of past falls and the imminence of more. When part of a glacier separates, the broken parts tend to be unstable. Along with the usual crevasses, vertical or tilting planes of ice form a jumble of towers, cliffs, and blocks, the whole comparable to the proverbial house of cards.

Risks obvious to the sophisticated eye tend not to endanger those with such an eye, just as knives and hammers do not require manufacturers' disclaimer warnings. But a few risks nonetheless go unrecognized or unnoticed. Benign surroundings induce complacency, which increases the risk.

A seductive menace, notorious for casualties, is level space beside the lip of a waterfall. The setting's picturesque charm—a view far off, a patch of grass among the trees beside smoothly flowing water that curves from sight—seems ideal for a picnic. Frolicking follows the sandwiches and juice, and maybe barefoot wading in the shallows, the slippery cliff forgotten. Doom awaits. Lord Byron wrote the following of an Alpine waterfall:

> *Lo! Where it comes like an eternity,*
> *As if to sweep down all things in its track,*
> *Charming the eye with dread, a matchless cataract,*
> *Horribly beautiful!*[33]

Which makes one wonder, what would he have written had he seen an avalanche?

At age thirty-one, John Muir clung to a wet ledge on the brink of Yosemite Falls, 3,000 feet above the valley floor. He wrote about his experience in *My First Summer in the Sierra*: "While perched on that narrow niche I was not distinctly conscious of danger. The tremendous grandeur of the

33. From "Childe Harold's Pilgrimage, Canto IV" (1818).

fall in form and sound and motion, acting at close range, smothered the sense of fear, and in such places one's body takes keen care for safety on its own account." Perhaps for John Muir, but the bodies of many of us neglect to protect us.

ACCIDENTS

Lots of falls do no harm. Others cause only minor injuries, such as ankle sprains.

A higher proportion of accidents are sustained among those on the way down from the top than among those either ascending or having turned back short of the summit. In part this owes to fatigue or impaired conditions (weather, snow, darkness). But to a substantial degree it owes to the lapse of concentration that comes with the assumption that an attained summit constitutes a completed task. This sense of completion is augmented by impatience and indifference toward a journey that is no longer a novel challenge. One's mind wanders to interests and concerns beyond one's hands and feet. Often those who descend neither beware of the way down nor provide for it in budgeting time and strength.

Denali statistics for most of the twentieth century show that 56 percent of fatalities among all climbers took place on descent. Most of these accidents were incurred by climbers high on the peak who were wobbling from fatigue, thin air, cold, and sometimes thirst. They slipped and then slid a long way, sometimes yanking off a companion. Although climbing falls are the most common cause of Denali's fatal accidents, the slip that sets off the fall is rarely the primary error that starts them. That earlier cause generally is the climber's weakened body and woozy mind after a few weeks of harsh conditions.

Records of mountaineering accidents in North America are interesting, yet they have little statistical value. Many accidents go unreported, and the reports that are filed don't include a measure of seriousness. Records of deaths, however, have some significance because almost all are reported and all have equal seriousness. There have been about 1,500 deaths in the second half of the twentieth century. For the decade 1963–72 there were 299 deaths, while for the decade 1991–2000 there were 354 deaths, an increase of about 18 percent over a period during which the number of mountaineers increased by far more than 18 percent. This suggests either that mountaineering has become less dangerous or that mountaineers have been tempting fate less often.

I have had my share of mountaineering accidents, but remain to tell of them. In the spring of 1982, after a failed try at the Emmons Glacier route on Rainier, I was on my way down the closed road from the ranger cabin to the White River campground. While trying to avoid a climber trio, I rode my bike into the ditch and cracked a right rib.

Four years later, further up the hill, I was coming down the Emmons after making the summit (my eighth try on that route). While crossing the 'schrund, an easy transition, I carelessly stumbled, took a somersault, sailed forth, and landed on my back on a thirty-five-degree slope. I bounced a couple of times and stopped. The next day, I descended from Camp Schurman and drove to the Swedish Hospital emergency room. I'd broken my left sixth rib. Its end permanently projects from my chest.

In 1977, climbing Silver Eagle Peak in the Alpine Lakes Wilderness area, I carelessly slipped while reaching for a hold, skidded a few yards, and hit the side of my head between temple and ear. I did not do any damage (but had a sore head that hurt when I chewed). In 1987, I took a long slide down a glacier on Johannesburg. The slide left a set of scrapes and bruises—more hazard than harm. And in 1991, when I was seventy-two, as Jim Wickwire and I were returning from a fine summer day's climb of Jabberwocky Tower, I took a careless header between boulders north of Colchuck Lake. The bleeding evoked an offer of first aid from Boy Scouts we passed. Each of these falls gave a disconcerting warning, though none did much harm. I've taken pride in the fact that after every injury, I've made my own way out of the mountains and driven myself to the hospital.

Some accidents make a heavy impact without harm to life or limb. High on the Denali West Ridge in 1980, socked in, as we paused for a snack and rest near a party of four or five, one in the party asked, "How far is it down there?" He was pointing into the fog, down the steep Wickersham Wall. I replied, "Oh my, it goes about forever—to the Peters Glacier." (This recalled Piglet's words to Pooh, "We'll be friends forever, won't we, Pooh?" and Pooh's response, "Even longer.") We looked more closely at these men and saw the face of one deeply forlorn, the others frustrated and angry. The sad one had let his pack slide from reach, losing enough of the party's supplies and equipment that they could not proceed. He may have been thinking, "For the next twenty years people in Denver will be telling each other, 'That's the schmuck who ruined his buddies' vacation when he threw his pack off some Alaskan peak.'"

Around 1947, in the rain on Squak Mountain, stumbling over logs, I fell on the hatchet I was carrying and sliced open the palm of my right hand, where the scar now offers a silent reminder of the folly. When I was skiing on Crystal Mountain in the 1950s, a somersault dislocated my right thumb, the eventual surgery leaving another scar. Two falls in the climbing gym in Seattle broke foot bones, first (ca. 1993) in the left, then (2002) in the right.

Peak climbing casualties are varied, while almost all rock-climbing casualties are falls—either the climber onto a rock or vice versa. One who leads on rock, meaning not a party's organizational leader but one who goes first on the rope while climbing, bears more risk. (In summit climbing, the difference in who goes first is slight.) As the saying goes, the leader takes "the sharp end of the rope." The primary difference in risk between the leader and one who "seconds" is the length—and its consequences—of a prospective fall. When a second slips, he falls the length of the slack in the rope, plus the stretch, which is short given the modest shock of the fall. This may be three to five feet. A secondary risk is the failure of the anchor by which the leader is belaying the second from above. Though the consequences of such a failure are usually fatal, the risk of it tends to be slight because the leader is expected to place a solid anchor for protection of both second and self.

Some leaders, more confident than prudent, skip opportunities for protections, setting them at longer intervals. A fall twenty feet above the last placement is long (forty feet), and at forty feet the acceleration makes it hard. Some leader falls are fatal because the leader climbs too far from his last protection. This may owe to recklessness or to ignorance of either the safe distance between protection points or the unavailability of protection on the route undertaken. As we hiked up to Ingalls Lake in 1979, my daughter

Margaret and I had wondered at a small plane circling above. Climber Fred Stanley and others in a mountain rescue group arrived and told us that a couple had been climbing the North Peak of Ingalls. While she belayed him from an anchor, he climbed, putting in no protection. On reaching the full rope length, he slipped. The slope was not vertical but was steep enough so that he took alternate bumps and falls until he had fallen twice the rope length and out of her sight.

On the second night after this fall, a man camped at the lake was awakened by cries from above. With a fine sense of responsibility, he rose, dressed, hiked out with a flashlight, drove to the ranger station, and reported this. The rescue team located the man's dead body, hanging below a ledge. At their request, I headed up to help recover the body, but came down again when this procedure was postponed. The man who found the woman, who had stayed put, afraid to try to descend alone, approached her hesitantly, fearing an abrupt reaction that might provoke a fall. When she saw him she asked, "How did he make out?" "He didn't make it." "That's what I figured." As she came off the peak and passed us, she looked composed.

A leader fall may be caused by the failure of a piece of protection that the climber has come upon but did not place himself. On an undertaking to climb Chumstick Snag a few miles off the Stevens Pass highway, when we had scrambled up to the first bolt, I put an index finger through it and gave a tentative pull. It came out in my hand. We three turned around and returned to the car.

I never broke a bone before age fifty-eight, but made up for that later: nine breaks, all from climbing. In June 1977, when my companion Allan Munro and I sought to climb Liberty Bell by the Beckey Crack, I forgot the way. After reaching the loose block above and to the left of the Fingertip Traverse, I went left instead of right, clinging to a horizontal crack without footholds below. After a desperate struggle to hold on until reaching easier holds, my grip came loose, followed by a drop of about fifteen feet. I landed on a sloping ledge, hurting something. I had neglected to take in the slack between myself and my belayer below.

I put in an anchor, rappelled down to Allan, and we did a series of rappels. After getting off the rock, I continued to rappel, using Allan as an anchor (he was bracing himself down the rock gully) and then using the trees into the basin. I made about a dozen rappels on the 150-foot rope at full length. This involved a lot of hopping backward on one foot. From the Blue Lake trail, Allan helped me much of the way with my arm over his shoulder. A minor factor along the trail was the worst harassment by mosquitoes that I had had in many a year. From the time I fell to getting to the car took nine hours. I drove home, arriving about 1:00 AM. The next day I proceeded to the emergency room, where I learned I'd sprained and fractured my right ankle. I spent seven weeks in a cast and then had bone fusion surgery the following year, which cured it. The failure to make the summit was discouraging. I would have much preferred to have fallen on the way down.

Ten years later, I went back and made the summit.

In the summer of 1991, I went off route while climbing Outer Space in the Cascades. I tried to do the crux with a lunge move, and got the usual result in such low-percentage moves: a fall, swinging into the wall. After three rappels to the foot of Snow Creek Wall, I got the rest of the way down by interminable hopping, helped by a stick. I drove back to Seattle, again to the emergency room (where one of the nurses recognized me as a frequent visitor), with a right ankle fracture and sprain.

Some leader falls that did me no harm scared me more than the falls that injured me. On Iguanarama in the West Cascades and Lightning Creek in the Peshastin Pinnacles, I came to rest upside down, with my head a few feet above a ledge.

Greg Child, one of the world's ablest and most experienced climbers, suffered a momentary lapse of attention when he rappelled off the rope ends far above the ground at Index in the Cascades and survived only by happening to fall through the shock-absorbent branches of a tree. Another escape was enjoyed in 2000 on Camelback Mountain in Arizona by a young man who caught himself in time on discovering that the ends of his rappel rope were 150 feet from the ground, possibly setting the world record for underestimating how much rope was needed for a rappel.

One uncommon risk is disproportionate, offsetting weights on a vertical rope. In 2000, a climber on El Cap in Yosemite, seeking to bring up his haul bag, stepped into space. But since he weighed 170 pounds and the bag 50 pounds, they both went zip, one upward and the other downward, and escaped disaster only by grace of a tangled rope. Once on a climb of Lexington, at Washington Pass, I began to fear that if I fell, my partner belaying me, fourteen-year-old Benjamin Silver, about two-thirds my weight, might be in for a sudden lift, with us passing each other like the weights in a cuckoo clock.

Sometimes the belayer's negligence is the source of the accident. The American Alpine Club reported that a girl had been leading a rock-climbing pitch, belayed by her father, when she asked to be lowered. He had let her down part of the distance to the ground where he stood when the rope that was passing through his belay device came to its end while she was still high above. Probably looking up at her, he had neglected his primary task and let the rope end slip through the device on his waist. His weight released from the rope that held her, he watched his daughter crater at his feet.

For survival, climbers now depend less on divine intervention or luck than in earlier years. Equipment now makes mountaineering far safer than in the early days. Of the mountaineering deaths in North America with reported causes, four times as many were attributed to lightning as to equipment failure. Of the few accidents caused by equipment failure, most are attributed to the human error of using impaired equipment such as a bent carabiner or a rope overdue to be put out to pasture.

Ropes no longer break (though a falling rock still may slice one). Ingenious hardware devices, both light and strong, can be fixed in a wide range of cracks, enabling attachment of rope to cliff to catch the climber who slips, thus shortening a fall. Rope, slings, and hardware (carabiners, rappel brakes, chocks, nuts, camming devices) are all made with a margin of strength beyond the shock that a fall sustains. On many routes where no natural objects—such as trees or cracks—are present to which to attach protection, bolts and rappel anchors have been placed in the rock along the way, enabling climbing without risk of a fatal fall.

Before these improvements, nothing could catch a fall. Now, however, if a rock climber "gets the chop" (as the colloquial term goes), his own fault—recklessness, carelessness, or negligence—is more probably the cause than bad luck or equipment failure.

SOLO ACCIDENTS

Solo climbing bears risk that varies from slight to suicidal, according to the relationship between the climber's skill, the route's difficulty, and the dependability of the holds. For solo climbing, as distinct from hiking alone in benign surroundings, risk rises along with satisfaction and thrill. Awareness that a slipped foot would open the gates of eternity keeps one on the qui vive and gives a satisfying sense of assuring one's own survival.

In the fall of 1980, I returned to Liberty Bell and tried to solo the Overexposure route. On the third pitch, I tied the rope end to my pack and left it on a ledge. With a length paid out and put through my belay device, I labored up the layback crack. Near the top I put in a couple of nuts and stood in slings clipped to them. With only a few feet left below a ledge on which to stand and rest, I lunged and surged upward, got my fingers on a hold, but lacked the strength to pull myself up further. My feet could not get a purchase on the slab. My fingers were tired, and the rock was cold in the shade. After a struggle, I slipped off, grabbed for the first sling, and missed. I got a piece of the second sling, which jerked from my hand. I thought: *With good luck, I will land squarely on the ledge, will not somersault forward, and likely will break a foot or two. With bad luck . . .* As it turned out, my luck was extra good. My belay partner, my pack, with the rope clipped to the upper nut, caught me about a foot from the ledge, so the rope stretch let me come down on my feet, but not hard. Chastened and shaken, grateful to have escaped harm, I gave up the chase, left the two nuts up there, pulled my rope back down, and rappelled. On the second and last rappel, a bottomless abyss below the anchor led me to swing over to one side, putting the rope behind a flake, to let myself down into the notch. Jammed behind the flake, the rope had to be left there. Elated by the sense of freedom and delight in the mountain surroundings, I headed down the hill in silent darkness, breathing the cool October air, the venture's exhilaration tempered by sober relief.

Twelve years later, I tried again. With improved skill from added experience, all went well. I felt I almost had it made. I got most of the way up the layback crack, holding on by the counterpressures of pushing forward with feet while pulling back on fingers curled over an edge of the crack. About three feet below the upper end of the crack (curiously, about where I had fallen before), where the ledge on which to rest awaited, the rope from my anchor below jerked up short. Having underestimated the distance to the next stance, I had not paid out enough slack. My response to this was to hold the layback with one hand, feet smearing the rock face, while with my other hand I tried to disconnect the knot from the locking biner on my seat harness for enough slack to make it up that last yard. The longer I fumbled, the more desperate my efforts and the more weary my other hand, clinging to the crack. As the strength in my left hand ebbed, I struggled on, ever more frantic, thus even more clumsy. At last my left-hand fingers turned to mush. I fell backward and, of course, down, first hitting a stub projecting from a small stump on the belay ledge, then bouncing off the ledge and coming to rest a few feet below, as the protection caught and held.

At seventy-three, I was old enough to know better. My guardian angel granted me the grace of good luck with only minor punishment for this folly. Among the multitude of dumb climbing mistakes over the past forty years, this was the worst (except possibly some mistakes not realized to be such because they went unpunished). Underestimating the length of rope needed to reach the ledge above was a mistake, but not serious or dumb. On getting caught short, I had three choices for letting out the needed slack: one would have been to climb back down to the anchor, extend the rope to let it reach the ledge above, then go up again. Another was to pop in a stopper and hang from it. Both were sensible. Either would have worked. But begrudging concession of the hard-earned vertical span, I did not down-climb, and failed to think of the second option. So I took the third. It had poor odds on success. If it failed, as it did, injury was a certainty. And were I to have managed to disconnect the rope at the moment of letting go of the crack, I would have been reminded, for one last moment, why the route is named Overexposure, as I fell into the chasm like John Milton's Lucifer, expelled from Heaven in the epic poem *Paradise Lost*:

> *from Morn*
> *To Noon he fell, from Noon to dewy Eve,*
> *A summer's day*

This may have been my narrowest escape in the mountains, although, of course, that moment may well have come unawares on any one of a number of casual occasions, whether strolling in the sunshine above a covered crevasse, or scrambling across a hillside on easy but precarious footing of snow or mud, above a bulge resembling the outside of a basketball.

I climbed back to the ledge, where I pulled myself together and gasped until I could take a deep breath. I did two rappels down to the notch (to one side of the abyss directly below), then a downward scuttle on the seat of my pants. Bellingham guys who had seen the fall carried my pack and rope and gave me a series of steadying belays as I descended the steep slope backward until reaching the trail. Pain and enfeeblement, combined with a chill wind, made their help gratifying during my gingerly shuffle down the trail. I drove back to town and to the hospital. Damage done: a couple of busted ribs, punctured and partly collapsed lung, and puncture hole in right thigh, leaving a permanent dimple, plus a few minor injuries. A long summer's day.

The next year I came back and made it, uneventfully. Although success was satisfying, an inner struggle denied pleasure in the process. My resolve not to be defeated pushed me upward, while my shaken nerve pulled me back.

WHITHER THE WEATHER

Weather provides mountaineers with discomfort, variety, and risk. Death from cold does not face rock climbers, except for those caught by a weather change while on a big-wall climb. But it significantly threatens peak climbers.

My only serious mountaineering injury from incidents other than falls was sustained on Denali in early May 1978. A couple of times I took off my mitts and gloves, and left them off too long while engaged in clumsy fumbling. The gloves got wet. We turned around at 19,700 feet in the dip between the Archdeacon's Tower and the Summit Dome, as I was stumbling and falling down every few steps. Result: frostbitten ten digits and three toes. I went to see a doctor in Anchorage who had vast experience with frostbite, his practice being located at the mouth of the (figurative) river down which flowed a multitude of frostbitten mountaineers. He advised me to check in at the hospital. Wanting to go home to Seattle, where I thought better care might be found, I had started to argue with him when his phone rang. He handed me a medical journal article he'd written and then answered his phone. The article was illustrated with revolting color photographs of frostbitten body parts. When he put down the phone, I said, "I'll go." After three days in the hospital I returned home, feeling self-pitying, decrepit, and futureless. My fingers and toes all stayed with me, but the punishment left a few reminders in the fingertips.

In the mountains, risk of lightning varies by location, as it does elsewhere. The risk is higher on top of an isolated tower, whether natural or manmade. Lightning takes rare victims but is more likely when one is clinging to something that, to a lightning bolt, might look like a lightning rod. Voytek Kurtyka and his partner were high on the Walker Spur in Antarctica when lightning struck both of them. Kurtyka's partner asked him his condition, and Voytek replied, "I okay. I only hit in head." One summer morning in the Cascades, under a low overcast, my companion Bill Glueck and I, on the second pitch of Prusik Peak's West Ridge, heard a shouted voice from above: "Big time static!" At that, we descended in haste, as did the pair above, while a thunderstorm began. Lightning struck the summit, and we were relieved that we had not risen half an hour earlier that day. Good judgment of what weather may come can help to reduce the odds of this type of accident.

Altitude sickness is a risk to all who climb to high altitude, since susceptibility cannot be forecast either by repeated past experience or by physical performance. In this it resembles seasickness. The probability of AMS (acute mountain sickness), HAPE (high-altitude pulmonary edema), or HACE (high altitude cerebral edema) befalling one is greatly increased by going up fast, rather than giving one's body time to acclimatize. Altitude sickness not only directly harms the body but also impairs capacity. Physically it can cause a climber to slip and fall or wearily sit down until he freezes on a chunk of snow. Mentally it can impair a climber's judgment, which can lead to disasters of other kinds. And, of course, high altitude impairs capacity even when it does not inflict a medical condition. British climber Eric Shipton wrote in his diary in 1938: "[A] climber on the upper part of Everest is like a sick man climbing in a dream."

Statistics on those who come to grief on Denali show a disproportionately large number who are hotshots from the Alps, many of them guides. Unfamiliar with an altitude almost a mile higher than Mont Blanc, yet strong and experienced, they have the capacity to climb fast and often do so, not having learned that acquiring the ability to breathe thin air will pay off on the final vertical feet. The high casualty rate from unfamiliar altitude effects is augmented by the vast glaciers, which produce giant crevasses that are often covered by huge snowfalls and made unstable by wild temperature swings.

Finally, it must be said that at *every* altitude, exhaustion tends to blur everything, whether looking outward or inward. This leads to mistakes, which in turn lead to harm.

PLAYING THE ODDS

Often you face hard choices when weighing risks, and good judgment may not be much help. Will safety increase by reducing speed or increasing it? Should you stop and take the ax from your pack when you come to a stretch of snow that calls for an ice ax in hand? Sure. But what if you're in a hurry, and the stretch is a gully only twenty feet wide? If the level of difficulty is barely at the point of calling for putting in protection, should you put in at the price of losing needed speed? On routes where retreat is not a possibility, you may have to choose between acting with haste to complete the route, thus increasing the risk of a fall, or taking care at a slow pace that increases the risk of being caught by weather or darkness.

When conditions endanger further upward effort, failure to cancel a climb and start descent tends to run the risk way up. The conditions may be thirst, fatigue, snowfall, storm, cold, or oncoming night. The temptation to incur this risk is greatest when the investment has been great and success is near—a journey laborious, hazardous, and long may be expensive to boot. Climbing into deteriorating weather offers bad odds, ranging from discomfort to disaster. Failure to turn back in time is caused in part by judgment error and in part by a failure of self-discipline.

Some people particularly vulnerable to this form of risk are those who seek to make just one big climb in their lives (the "one big climb" syndrome).

Their competitive motive may be as much external as internal—that is, they are competing for the approval of non-climbers. They have climbed little and expect to climb little more, but seek one big score with which to notch their belts. They often take substantial risks because they do not calibrate risk with the precision that experience brings. Their longing to make the summit suppresses their prudence, which may be telling them to turn back even though they are so near their goal. Such a person, having gotten himself to 20,000 feet, may be hard to deter from tottering and gasping on, even in the face of his declining condition and that of his surroundings, both of which indicate low survival odds. To such an individual, the day's summit may matter more than to one who knows he will have other days to try and thus turns back at wet rock, unstable snow, fatigue, oncoming night, or conditions that foretell an avalanche or storm. One who feels he may return again and again more readily chooses to turn around 200 yards from the top.

A variation on this syndrome was illustrated by Dainius Makauskas's behavior on Dhaulagiri, the seventh-highest peak in the world, located in Nepal. He so strongly wanted to become the first Lithuanian to make the summit of an 8,000-meter peak that he took irresponsible risks. He had injured his knee, yet went on. Before heading up, anticipating that he might not survive, he sorted his belongings into two packages and designated one for each of his two adoring sons. He reached the summit, but succumbed on his way down.

A climber in the grip of the "one big climb" syndrome, feeling that the short remaining way to the goal offers much improved odds, resembles the oil driller who has put a fortune into a dry hole and is tempted to put in his last dollars to drill a few feet more. Some, with an even worse measurement of odds, buy one more lottery ticket after many that did not win. I have committed this error repeatedly. In 1988, I started up the east face of Vasiliki Tower in the North Cascades. The angle steepened until I felt insecure, but I kept on to the summit. I was reluctant to waste the time and effort taken to get to the point where prudence directed me to retreat. I wish I could say I never made this error again, but I did.

Those for whom risk appeals in and of itself, or those who are indifferent to risk, may be more inclined to experiment. According to studies, many such individuals are later-born sons. Those who put a high value on the reward, however, either as a competitor or as a matter of principle, are willing to take the risk to gain the reward. Many such individuals are women or firstborn sons. Other things being equal, women climbers enjoy or accept a lesser degree of risk than men. Women who do take high risks, therefore, tend to demand a higher reward than do men.

Many climbers find both risk and reward appealing. English mountaineer Leslie Stephen, as quoted by Fergus Fleming in *Killing Dragons*, declared: "There is perhaps some pleasure in being killed trying to do what has never been done before; but there is no pleasure in being killed in simply following other people's footsteps. . . . No advertisement of Alpine adventure is so attractive as a clear demonstration that it is totally unjustifiable."

Each mountaineer sets his degree of risk, according to an inner equation, by choices of where and when to go. For a rock climb, the choice depends on how close to the edge one is willing to push the limits of one's own climbing capacity. For objective dangers, the choice is made by measuring the hazards of the mountains.

Risk can be increased by momentum from a series of prior decisions, each of which increased a bit, so that when the climber faces another risk-taking choice he feels pushed by the past chain to take one more incremental step. It can also be increased by competitiveness or ambition, the latter of which is a longer-range version of the former. Competition induces a climber to measure his performance against a standard set by companions, by past records, or by the prospect of his achievement entering route guides, journals, or books. Or possibly he has set the standard wholly by and for himself.

The greatest single class of risk-takers is youthful, energetic enthusiasts who assume that death, if it ever must come, is just for old folks. Their high spirits and innocence make them fail to recognize risks for what they are. As Joseph Conrad reflected in his short story *Youth*:

> *And I remember my youth and the feeling that will never come back*
> *any more—the feeling that I could last forever, outlast the sea, the*
> *earth, and all men; the deceitful feeling that lures us on to joys, to*
> *perils, to love, to vain effort—to death; the triumphant conviction of*

strength, the heat of life in the handful of dust, the glow in the heart
that with every year grows dim.

There are also climbers for whom risk is meaningless. They are sunk in despair, and climb for oblivion through exhaustion, or to put themselves out on the edge to recover a lost sense of power or worth. Indifferent to living, they are indifferent to risk.

A few years ago, after a Rainier guide had enjoyed a blissful weekend with a colleague, his romantic visions turning to a vine-covered cottage and the patter of little feet, he broached plans for how they would spend the next weekend together. His companion, attractive but with a short emotional attention span, explained that she would be occupied with another man. A couple of days later, the disappointed young man, climbing Pinnacle Peak (a little south of Paradise Lodge) alone, fell to his death.

Late one summer afternoon, as I strolled among the Enchantment Lakes, a friendly acquaintance came around a corner. He carried a light day pack and no climbing gear. I asked him what he'd done that day, to which he replied, "The so-and-so route on Colchuck Peak, the so-and-so route on Dragontail (both technical climbs), and the South Face of Prusik." As to the last, a 5.9, 10-pitch climb on a peak without a nontechnical descent route, I asked him how he had come down, and he said he had down-climbed the rappel route. Later, a mutual friend told me that this remarkable day's performance had been set off by receipt of a Dear John letter.

Then come those who are obsessed, driven by a compulsion to score one route or summit after another, never satisfied by what they have done. Among them, however, like those obsessed with making money, are some who couple obsession with caution, limiting the risks they take. Without such constant caution, which he acquired over the years, luck alone would not have enabled Fred Beckey to make challenging climbs sixty years after he started.

Some who belong near this point on the scale are addicted to risk. They would rather take a high wire than a high road. After the wife of leading British mountaineer Alan Burgess caught him in an affair, he wrote in *The*

Burgess Book of Lies: "I had risked Daphne's and my relationship, more for the risk itself than anything else. I enjoyed living on the edge and had confused my rebellious attitude toward mountains with a feeling of being trapped."

Some mountaineers are prompted by the reverse of a suicidal impulse. Appetite for life and hunger for engagement make them want to live forever. They exult in using their bodies to the fullest and without knowing what experience lies ahead. This intensity and acceptance of uncertainty come not from desperation or indifference but from zest. Such climbers prefer to measure the quality of experience and level of achievement by difficulty rather than by uncontrollable danger. An episode in which the latter intrudes itself provokes disgust rather than exhilaration; it impairs rather than enhances a climb. The risks taken are not ends in themselves, but incidental consequences of full engagement, of living on all cylinders. Those who love life give the risks more heed.

The odds on each horse in a horse race do not reflect objective probability, since they are not based on the results of similar random events. Rather, they reflect the combined subjective probability in the minds of all who place bets, and thus tend to be more realistic. In a similar way, probability has use for a mountaineer, who can look at the success and failure rates of others on a given route to determine probability for himself. In mountaineering, one cannot isolate risks. They all affect each other. But that is the case in most of life, except, say, in a game of pure chance.

A mountaineer makes decisions about risk much as most people make decisions when the consequences are uncertain: by relating, measuring, offsetting, and balancing not only possibilities and probabilities but also desires, dislikes, hopes, and fears. When considering whether to undertake a given climb, the mountaineer frames, examines, and seeks to solve an equation that embodies the factors that will affect his choice. He measures the gravity of the harm, the appeal of the reward, and the odds of the result. No mountaineer has been known to work out an explicit equation of this kind, but many do weigh the foregoing factors in reaching their decision. In varying proportions, this process is conscious and unconscious. Some, of course, give this matter no thought.

For a dangerous and difficult climb, a mountaineer in effect places a bet—say, one-third to win, meaning to succeed in the intended climb. That bet would also mean two-thirds odds of losing, meaning not to succeed. Those odds on losing might be broken down to $1/150$ to be killed, and $99/150$ to fail but survive. This contrasts with a money bet, where money states the terms of either a win or a loss. In a mountaineering bet, losing may not be altogether a form of loss, because a failed summit may offer some positive experience to offset the disappointment of failure.

Of course, every mountaineering casualty (except those—largely hypothetical—due to suicide or crime) contains at least some element of bad luck. And some escapes from disaster may be attributed to astounding good luck. Greg Child was saved by going through tree branches; Rébuffat and Lachenal were tumbling together down a steep, high Alp when their rope caught on a knob; noted climber and author David Roberts and his partner on Mount Huntington were caught by a knob "about the size of one's knuckle" as recorded in his collection *Moments of Doubt*.

An example of what was perhaps one-tenth error followed by nine-tenths luck, first good, then bad, took place in the spring of 1978 when American climbers Galen Rowell and Ned Gillette were passing Windy Corner on their way up Denali. They concluded that prudence called for shifting from cross-country skis to crampons. In Rowell's later-published words, while engaged in their transfer of equipment, Gillette slipped and "fell toward an ice cliff only sixty feet below. About forty feet of rope was between us. My ice axe was still on my pack, so I made a hasty self-arrest with the base of a ski pole. An instant later I was jerked from my stance and shot across the ice. . . . [W]e were both headed for a last, long ride."[34] Gillette managed to grab a bit of rubbish, a dangling strand of an old fixed rope, and came to a stop, "three feet short of the lip of the cliff," hanging upside down. Rowell landed on his partner headfirst, and one of Gillette's skis slashed Rowell's face so that when my Seattle climbing partner Bill Sumner, Jim Wickwire, and I came upon him at an airfield near Anchorage, he looked like a student just initiated into a Heidelberg fraternity.

34. From "Up and Around Mount McKinley," *American Alpine Journal* (1979).

For all kinds of mountaineering, it's possible to miscalculate the odds on the kind of risk that effort or skill cannot avoid, so that you accept odds worse than you wish to take. Since the principal rock-climbing risk is concentration lapse, a climber must measure the odds of forgetting to pay attention. Robert Graves made the same point in his autobiography: "Rock-climbing, one of the most dangerous sports possible, unless he keeps to the rules, becomes reasonably safe if he does keep to them."

Some become incredibly lucky despite miscalculating their personal formula of cost, reward, and odds. Others suffer misfortune despite wholly accurate measurements, and are done in by the throw of the dice. Over the long run, of course, those who miscalculate tend not to attain their pursued ends. When a group of four of us failed to reach the top of the North Cascades' Nooksack Tower, we dragged back to our bivouac well after midnight. While three of us subsided on our backs, Rimas Gylys, wishing to avoid a late return to his job in Canada, headed downward with a flashlight. A week later, a searcher found his corpse at the foot of a cliff. He had punched through a clump of brush that hid the lip. The strongest climber among us, he had made an unsound calculation of his formula, although one cannot know whether he had given excessive weight to punctuality at work, assigned insufficient weight to extending life, or mistaken the odds on a faint-trail descent in the dark.

For rational decisions about risk, the factors of cost and reward are given their *subjective* value by the decision-maker. The more dinner in your stomach, the less you value the next forkful. For one with a life expectancy of one year, death presents—or should present—a lower cost than it does to one with a fifty-year expectancy. A prospective reward of $10,000 is worth less to one who is worth millions than it is to a beggar. Most lottery tickets are bought by people who can ill afford them, just as most of the Klondike prospectors, who underwent such toil, hardship, and personal risk, were poor men.

Often, risks are not easily foreseeable by the participants, so error may be hard to attribute. In 1971, I climbed Rainier by the Gibraltar route, the fourth on a rope with two other middle-aged lawyers, both vigorous men but inexperienced mountaineers, and my fourteen-year-old son. This was a direct and easy climb, with some entertainingly eerie phenomena as we skirted the foot of the great overhanging cliff—slimy rock, water dripping on us, a few thunderous rockfalls nearby in the dark (not threatening, because they came from above the overhang). A bit above this, however, where we front-pointed with our crampons for a few hundred feet, our companion in the lead failed to slow down and cut steps. The angle and hard, slick snow made self-arrest improbable if one slipped, so any of the four might have jerked the rest off, with death waiting below. For me, awareness of this risk did not sink in until the slope had eased. In retrospect, I've been uncertain what I should have done, and when.

The next morning, as I was biking down Pike Street in Seattle on my way to work, I fell off my bike going over a divider bump, but escaped with no more than bruises and torn pants. A few days later I sprained my ankle tripping on the carpet at the office. These events reminded me that, as in law, medicine, war, and many other walks of life, one can safely assert the proposition that risk is where you find it and often occurs when neither anticipated nor even imagined.

Another example of odds is the question that may face a climber about to put a rappel rope through an anchor previously set in the cliff: a pair of bolts connected by a chain, with one end of the chain attached by a big ring. The question: Whether to run the rope over the chain or to put it through the big ring.

If the rope is put over the chain, the number of links multiplies the chance that one link will break. The longer the chain, the more those chances; yet as the two sections of the chain approach a parallel, the pull on each bolt is reduced toward half the pull on the rope. If, however, the chain follows a straight horizontal line between the bolts (reflecting a badly-created anchor), the pull on the chain generates a tension on each bolt far greater than half the pull on the rope. And it also generates a strain on the chain itself. If the rope is put over the chain and either bolt pulls out, the rope slides off the end. Thus the anchor fails either if any link in the chain breaks or if either bolt pulls out. The odds are bad enough in that situation to make the choice of avoiding it an easy one.

If the rope is run through the big ring, there are comparative disadvantages: All the weight pulls on one bolt. The weight is not shared. This disadvantage is partially offset by the fact that, if the bolt pulls out, the ring remains on the end of the chain attached to the other bolt, which may save the day, but the weight shifts in a jerk that greatly increases the strain. An offsetting comparative advantage is that the ring is bigger than the chain links, so it is less likely to break than any link and not subject to the chances being multiplied by the number of links. As long as the ring and the links stay intact, the anchor does not fail unless both bolts pull out.

Lest the lay reader visualize the climber pondering the complex and interrelated odds as the sun sinks low and companions shout to get on with it, two things may be kept in mind. Artificial rappel anchors tend to be built with an excess margin of strength, and the question may well be decided by the climber giving each bolt a heave to see if it can be uprooted.

A simpler example of a choice to improve one's odds is to add another piece of protection to an anchor—two pieces instead of one or three instead of two. This is the principle of "belt and suspenders": either measure may let your pants drop, but using both improves your odds.

Still another aspect of a mountaineer's calculus of risk is adjusting to conclusions reached by one's companions in *their* calculations. On descent from Exfoliation Dome, which my companion and I had not climbed before, darkness overtook us with what seemed to be a couple of rappels left to go. My companion, combining hedonism with supreme optimism, urged continuing, but I declined to budge, so we hung there till early morning light showed he had been right—in the sense that the ends of the rope below us actually reached footing solid and safe.

BELT AND SUSPENDERS

One may manage risk by reducing it or shifting it. Mountains and mountaineers being what they are, managing mountaineering risk by spreading it simply won't do. Reducing it often will. Edward Whymper, the British mountaineer most known for his first ascent of the Matterhorn, said as his closing words in his book about the climb:

> *Climb if you will, but remember that courage and strength are*
> *naught without prudence, and that a momentary negligence may*

destroy the happiness of a lifetime. Do nothing in haste, look well to
each step, and from the beginning think what may be the end.

Since negligence causes most rock-climbing accidents, the risk of a momentary lapse of concentration may be reduced to a reassuring minimum by
practicing each customary and correct procedure until it becomes habit, and
therefore less often neglected.

These procedures include belaying, checking and rigging anchors, putting in protection, rappelling, and attaching rope to harness and harness
to self. When Marty Hoey slipped off a ledge, her unfastened belt let her
fall out of her harness—and fall off Mount Everest. More than once, on
taking long enough falls to warrant a hard jerk, I've come to a stop hanging head down, grateful that my harness was tight enough that I did not
pull out of it.

On rock, one can sharply and consistently reduce risk by confining one's
climbs to well-protected or protectable routes and by doing no lead climbing. If you climb only with a rope extending above yourself, you are far less
likely to suffer injury from a fall, yet you can do climbs of difficulty equal
to, or greater than, what you could do if you led them. Likewise, one can
increase risk by choosing to climb solo, go to higher altitude or looser rock,
or climb in a place or season of greater cold, more frequent avalanches, or
more severe storms.

One risk mountaineers cannot escape is financial. A person who climbs
with a professional guide must execute a comprehensive disclaimer, agree-
ing not to hold the guide liable for injuries caused by the guide's negligence.
And when members of a climbing party have no commercial or professional
relationship, the victim of a leader fall cannot hope to recover on a claim
against the belayer whose negligence let the rope run out; it is recognized that
the leader assumed such risk. Some activities, such as driving an automo-
bile, removing an appendix, or maintaining the floor of a store, are common
enough for the law to have developed rulings and rules that establish standards of care. And the surrounding circumstances often enable an accurate
measurement of what happened. Not so in climbing. And the impossibility
of measuring risks makes insurance companies unwilling to place any bets.

On the subject of finances, I've often pondered how to allocate fairly the costs incurred by rescue organizations. A rescue may involve a helicopter that lifts someone off a peak, or a volunteer band that responds to a call by meeting at the trailhead at midnight. The volunteers then heave packs to shoulders and head up the hill. How should the cost of rescue and medical care be divided between the taxpayers and those who are helped or wish to be eligible for help if needed?

In the Alps, the full cost of rescue tends to be borne by the government. In part that reflects the high proportion of locals who climb their mountains, in contrast to most other countries, and in part it constitutes a subsidy to the important business of tourism.

These are a puzzling set of questions. Should all rely on the service of voluntary rescue groups that have become well established in some areas? Should public agencies, using public funds, undertake to rescue all who need it? Should those who undertake a climb that involves more risk than a hike in the sunshine be required to pay a premium on an insurance policy that would cover average rescue costs?

These questions remain unanswered. Interestingly, however, many serious mountaineers practice a form of risk management by what they do when out of the mountains, such as improving the odds on health by limiting cigarettes, alcohol, and weight gain. Greg Child remarked: "Maybe Himalayan climbing is just a bad habit, like smoking, of which one says with cavalier abandon, 'Must give this up someday, before it kills me.'" When I became a climber, I stopped riding a motorcycle, concluding that this exceeded my risk quota.

The mountaineer may calculate that the climbing risks to which he exposes himself are, in part, offset by avoiding some risks of home life, where so many people suffer injuries that at least are disabling. For instance, the surefootedness acquired from a mountaineer's time in the hills reduces his risk of falls from stairs or landings, the leading cause of death in the home. (And there is no evidence that hubris offsets this reduced risk by inducing climbers to recklessly dash downstairs.) The comparative odds are further improved by the comparative time exposure—say twenty years of high-energy mountaineering compared with a lifetime of dangers of lowlands life.

CONCLUSION

· · · · ·

Illusion Dweller

A GOAL BECKONED.

I wanted to lead a beautiful crack route, given five-star quality, on a cliff north of Palm Springs, California. The route's captivating name: Illusion Dweller. Several developments prompted this desire. My body would no longer let me hike far uphill, so peaks were out. Although the rock route would be harder than any that I had done, it was conceivably doable, and it had to be tried forthwith before my capacity further declined. At age eighty-three, a future chance was foreclosed. And I had an impulse to achieve a last score, as Tennyson's Ulysses exhorted his comrades:

> *Some work of noble note may yet be done,*
> *Not unbecoming men that strove with gods.*

I exercised, practiced, got my weight down to what it was at age eighteen, and took trips to Joshua Tree National Park to struggle up the route, protected by a top rope. My body could do each move, but my stamina would give out and my confidence was low. Halfway up, I'd be exhausted. After each attempt, I would come down so sunk in discouragement that I would decide to give up. Then, after a day, I would cheer up and renew aim and effort.

This 5.10b route obsessed me. Brooding by day, stewing by night, week after week, I daydreamed of climbing it. I began to wonder: Is this pesky Illusion Dweller, this cracked cliff, running my life? Is its name my condition? Are our roles reversed? The question suggested the French Renaissance writer Montaigne's rumination about how he enjoyed playing with his cat but sometimes wondered whether, in fact, his cat was playing with him. Or what about Lao Tzu, who one night dreamed he was a butterfly, and the rest of his life was perplexed by the question: Was he a philosopher dreaming he was a butterfly, or a butterfly dreaming it was a philosopher?

Then the time came to have at it. Most of this long, single-pitch route is a diagonal crack. At first, it was thin. Fingers were stuck in as far as they would go—not far. Feet would do their best to get a purchase by smearing against the cliff, and seeking to take advantage of any irregularity on which friction could be obtained by a downward push. Further up, the crack widened enough to jam in one's hands. One hand would hold much of one's weight, while the other moved up to another jam. As best fitted the details of the crack and the position of one's body, a hand would be placed thumb up or thumb down. Along this stretch one often could jam a toe into the crack, although the diagonal to the level pushed the other foot out onto the face. As the crack expanded further, one's hands were curled into fists, which were jammed. One's foot or feet could also be inserted and leaned on. Both jammed fists and inserted feet were twisted, to increase the pressure and consequent friction on the sides of the crack. There followed a stretch where the crack was a bit wider, and one of its edges provided a sharp enough corner for "layback" moves, for which one would lean out to one side, fingers curled over the edge of the crack, while feet pressed against the wall or the other side of the crack, with offsetting pressure—much as fingers and thumb can hold a glass, while neither can do so alone. At the top came the crux, an overhang. Knowledge that victory was at hand—though out of sight above the roof—supplied added energy, needed for the struggle up these last moves.

Gasping, I squirmed for the finish and wriggled onto the ledge. The triumph was satisfying. I also had the tempering reflection that I'd been gratified by something more fitting for the young.

When I untied on top, before scrambling down the easier back side, my first feeling was no more than modest pride. I also felt enormous relief at not having to do that thing ever, ever, ever again.

| INDEX |

OTHER TITLES YOU MIGHT ENJOY
FROM MOUNTAINEERS BOOKS

THROUGH A LAND OF EXTREMES
The Littledales of Central Asia
Elizabeth and Nicholas Clinch
The adventures of a largely forgotten Victorian couple who made some of the most amazing expeditions of their day, including nearly reaching the forbidden city of Lhasa.

THE ROSKELLEY COLLECTION
Stories Off the Wall, Nanda Devi, and Last Days
John Roskelley
Together in one volume for the first time, the writings of one of America's premier—and most outspoken—climbers.

A LIFE ON THE EDGE
Memoirs of Everest and Beyond
Jim Whittaker
The fiftieth anniversary edition of Jim Whittaker's memoir, with full-color photographs and a new final chapter.

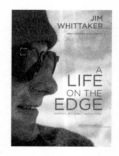

EVEREST

The West Ridge

Thomas Hornbein

The fiftieth anniversary edition of Thomas Hornbein
and Willi Unsoeld's first glory-or-death ascent of
Everest's West Ridge, with never-before-published
expedition photographs and a new foreword by Jon
Krakauer.

ON BELAY

The Life of Legendary Mountaineer Paul Petzoldt

Raye Ringholz

An intimate biography of the most cherished and
controversial icon of outdoor leadership in the United
States.

**MOUNTAINEERS
BOOKS**

1001 SW Klickitat Way, Suite 201 • Seattle, WA 98134
800-553-4453 • mbooks@mountaineersbooks.org • www.mountaineersbooks.org

LEGENDS AND LORE SERIES

The Legends and Lore series was created by Mountaineers Books in order to ensure that mountaineering literature will continue to be widely available to readers everywhere. From mountaineering classics to biographies of well-known climbers, and from renowned high-alpine adventures to lesser-known accomplishments, the series strives to bring mountaineering knowledge, history, and events to modern audiences in print and digital form.

All Legends and Lore titles are made possible through sales of Mountaineers Books titles, special events, and the generosity of donors. Mountaineers Books would like to thank the following individuals for contributing to the Legends and Lore series of books:

- Tom Hornbein
- Tina Bullitt
- William Sumner
- Alex Bertulis
- Anonymous

To donate, purchase books, or learn more, visit us online at www.mountaineersbooks.org.

MOUNTAINEERS BOOKS